G000255176

SCAPEGOAT

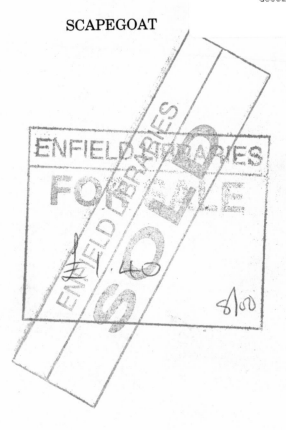

ENFIELD LIBRARIES
FOR SALE
SOLD
ENFIELD LIBRARIES
£1.40

SCAPEGOAT

*The inside story
of the trial of Derek Bentley*

JOHN PARRIS

Duckworth

First published in 1991
Gerald Duckworth & Co. Ltd.
The Old Piano Factory
48 Hoxton Square, London N1 6PB

© 1991 by Evradean Ltd

All rights reserved. No part of this publication
may be reproduced, stored in a retrieval system, or
transmitted, in any form or by any means, electronic,
mechanical, photocopying, recording or otherwise,
without the prior permission of the publisher.

A catalogue record for this book is available
from the British Library

ISBN 0 7156 2357 5

Photoset in North Wales by
Derek Doyle & Associates, Mold, Clwyd.
Printed in Great Britain by
Redwood Press Limited, Melksham

London Borough
of Enfield
Public Libraries

8/91

008301175

345 ·02523

Contents

To the memory of
His Honour Sir Rudolph Lyons QC
1912–1991

Plates

(between pp. 128 and 129)

Christopher Craig (The Hulton Picture Company).

Derek Bentley (The Hulton Picture Company).

The scene of the crime: Barlow & Parker's warehouse roof.

Christopher Craig at Croydon Magistrates' Court.

John Parris, counsel for Craig.

Frank Cassels, counsel for Bentley.

Christmas Humphreys, counsel for the Crown.

Rayner Goddard, Lord Chief Justice of England.

PC Sidney Miles, shot dead on Barlow & Parker's warehouse roof, 2 November 1952 (Popperfoto).

DCI John Smith (The Hulton Picture Company).

DC Frederick Fairfax, PC James McDonald and PC Norman Harrison (The Hulton Picture Company).

Mr and Mrs Craig leaving the Old Bailey during the trial (The Hulton Picture Company).

Mr and Mrs Bentley and their daughter Iris visit Derek Bentley under sentence of death in Wandsworth Prison (The Hulton Picture Company).

Sydney Silverman MP (Popperfoto).

Sir David Maxwell Fyfe, Home Secretary (Popperfoto).

A crowd of demonstrators at the gates of Wandsworth Prison on 28 January 1953, as an official tries to post the notice of execution of Derek Bentley (Popperfoto).

The goat, on which the lot fell to be the scapegoat, shall be presented alive before the LORD, to make an atonement with him, and to let him go for a scapegoat into the wilderness. ...

And when he hath made an end of reconciling the holy place, and the tabernacle of the congregation, and the altar, he shall bring the live goat:

And Aaron shall lay both his hands upon the head of the live goat, and confess over him all the iniquities of the children of Israel, and all their transgressions in all their sins, putting them upon the head of the goat, and shall send him away by the hand of a fit man into the wilderness:

And the goat shall bear upon him all their iniquities into a land not inhabited: and he shall let go the goat in the wilderness.

Leviticus 16:10, 20-22

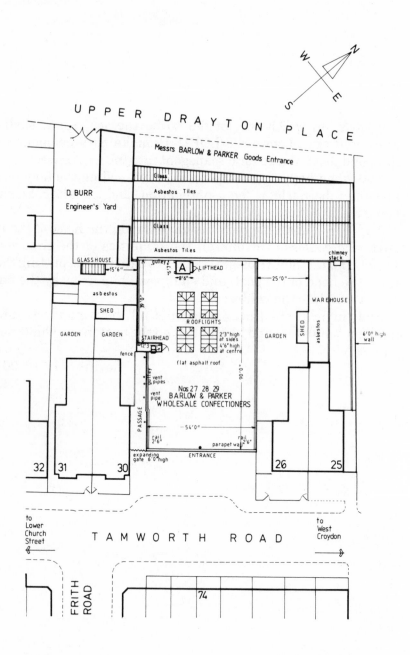

Plan of Barlow & Parker's Warehouse. Drawn by Graham Caswell

10

1

Brief for the Defence

It was a Sunday afternoon in November 1952, a wintry but sunny day, but with patches of fog floating past the windows. My wife, Joyce, and I had been to Matins at St George's Church, Leeds and come back to our house in Alwoodley for the conventional Sunday midday dinner of roast beef – 'a corner cut of hinderbone' – Yorkshire pudding, baked potatoes and brussels sprouts, followed by a spotted dick pudding.

In those distant days we always had a live-in maid, invariably a daughter of a miner, from South Yorkshire or Durham. We even had an electric button under the carpet in the dining room, so that I could press it and a bell in the kitchen would tell her when to serve the next course. But it was Sunday and when the girl had served the meal and washed up, it was her day off. So we were alone in the house.

I was dozing in a blue uncut moquette armchair by the fire when the phone rang. It was on the floor beside me and I lifted it reluctantly, still half asleep.

It was my clerk.

'I've been trying to get you all yesterday afternoon and evening,' he said testily.

'We went to a matinee at White Rose Players in Harrogate and then had dinner at a nice little Italian Restaurant that's just opened there.'

'No wonder you're always behind with your paper work,' he said in the tone of voice that a farmer might well use to a cow whose milk yield had diminished. 'After you left Chambers yesterday I had a call from a London solicitor to retain you as junior for the defence of Craig.'

'Craig? Who's he?'

'Don't you read the papers?'

'Not on Sundays.'

'The papers have been full of it. Christopher Craig is a teenage kid who has shot and killed a copper in Croydon.'

'Poor Person's Defence, I suppose?'

*

In those days there was no legal aid, and counsel were expected to appear for those without funds for a fee of three guineas – unless, of course, it was a dock brief, when the fee was one guinea. My clerk, in the mysterious way of barristers' clerks, was astute at getting me out of court whenever some prisoner was proposing to ask for a dock brief.

'Don't worry,' he said. 'You're going to be led by Derek Curtis Bennett, and all you'll have to do will be take a note. You won't have to open your mouth.'

'But it'll cost me the earth in expenses.'

'It'll be good experience to appear at the Old Bailey with Curtis Bennett. He's the tops in criminal defence. I've accepted the brief.'

I put the phone down and went to look at my unread pile of copies of *The Times*. We did not have a television then. (Nor do I now, thirty-eight years later.) The last couple of weeks had been such that I had no time even to glance at the papers. Up early, some days to drive to York or Hull. Conference after court to return home for dinner at nine and then sit up till one o'clock in the morning drafting pleadings and writing opinions. Two weeks after the crime had been committed I had never heard of Christopher Craig or his partner in crime, Derek Bentley.

In those days *The Times* carried small advertisements on its front page, as it had done since its first issue. I had some difficulty therefore in finding its reports about the case. Two youths, one 16 and the other 19, had apparently been attempting to break into a warehouse in Croydon when the police were alerted and surrounded the place. The 16-year-old,

1. Brief for the Defence

Christopher Craig, had drawn a gun and shot two police officers, one fatally.

I read the reports and we then went off to the Red Lion at South Stainley, near Harrogate, to have afternoon tea of cucumber sandwiches and cream cakes with strawberry jam, served by elderly waitresses in mop caps, black dresses and white pinafores. The then elegant inn was packed out. It was the fashionable thing to do in Yorkshire in 1952, although it would no doubt have incurred the displeasure of my clerk had he known, as a diversion from my primary function in life: to earn fees for him.

In those days, I did not take the *Daily Mail*, any more than I do now. It, I understand, had headlines:

CHICAGO GUN BATTLE
IN LONDON: GANGSTERS
WITH MACHINE GUNS
ON ROOF KILL
DETECTIVE, WOUND
ANOTHER

and copy under which read:

The London crime wave reached a new peak last night. A detective was shot dead and another seriously wounded in a second 'Battle of Sidney Street'.

They had seen the flash of a torchlight in the warehouse of Barlow and Parker, wholesale confectioners, Tamworth Road, Croydon, just after ten o'clock. They entered the building. They cautiously edged their way in. Inside the raiders were so far undisturbed. Ambulances and fire brigades had been summoned.

Then as the bandits realised they had been trapped by a police cordon, shooting began. The gangsters armed with a Sten-gun hit one of the officers as he climbed the fire escape towards the bandits. He was Detective Constable Miles, in plain clothes of Z Division, a married man with two children with 12 years service. He was killed.

His colleague, PC Frederick Fairfax, who was in a police patrol car, dashed into an alleyway leading to another fire escape up which the gunman had climbed. He fell wounded in the shoulder.

The report had at least twenty-five errors of fact, which I suppose is a fair average for any report in the *Daily Mail*. It was, however, typical of the sort of prejudicial propaganda against the two accused which was then flooding the popular press and which made it almost impossible to find a jury whose minds had not been warped by what they had read about them.

This is still an unresolved problem. The Irish government rightly refused to extradite an Irish priest to the United Kingdom after Mrs Thatcher, then Prime Minister, had, before the trial, repeatedly denounced him as guilty. There was no prospect whatsoever of his receiving a fair trial in England – if anybody ever does. Jurors can be told to put out of their minds whatever they have previously read, but this is like asking them to remove their own skin. What they have read and the conclusions they have drawn become part of their own bodies.

*

As it happened, I was not to be led by Curtis Bennett. The magistrates were so incensed with the wickedness of the crime committed by the accused that, instead of granting, as was then invariably the practice in murder trials, a certificate for two counsel, they granted each a certificate for one only.

So far from only having to take a note and not open my mouth, I found myself charged with the burden of defending the youth who had done the killing.

When it became known that I was to be the sole counsel to defend Craig, there was some curiosity as to why I, an obscure barrister from obscure chambers in Leeds, who had been in practice for a mere four years, should be chosen to lead for the defence in what journalists were already terming 'the trial of the century'. Most Londoners believe civilisation ends at Potter's Bar.

1. Brief for the Defence

It was some time before I found out, from Christopher Craig himself, how I had come to be briefed.

2

Chambers in Leeds

In 1990 the Bar Council produced a report, *Strategies for the Future*, prepared for it by the accountants Coopers & Lybrand. In it barristers are advised to develop 'marketing and promotional programmes': i.e. to advertise and publicise their talents. They are recommended to locate themselves in provincial centres as close as possible to the source of their work.

Things change. In 1952 it was the greatest crime against professional etiquette to make any attempt to publicise yourself. I was twice charged before the Grand Court of the North Eastern Circuit with this grave crime. Both charges were entirely false and on both occasions I was exonerated.

In 1952 the 'Provincial Bar' was despised and treated with contempt by all the Oxbridge types who occupied subsidised chambers in the Inns of Court, who lunched or dined every day with the judges and who, inevitably, were the only ones considered for important judicial appointments.

*

Our chambers at No. 38 Park Square, Leeds consisted of the ground-floor front room of a Georgian house and a narrow room behind which may once have been the kitchen and which was just big enough to house two desks, one for the clerk and the other for the typist.

They were far from popular with the North Eastern Circuit. In the first place, for one reason or another none of the members had been away on war service; secondly, and at a time when

17

there was an acute shortage of counsel, they had made an immense amount of money. The clerk who had been there during this period, and who was still clerk when I arrived in 1947, had made so much that shortly afterwards he went off and bought a 58-bedroom hotel in the Isle of Wight, paying cash down. On top of that, the chambers continued to be immensely successful after the war.

But even worse was the fact that some of the members of our chambers before I arrived had not been to public school. Most were the products of Leeds Grammar School and Leeds University and were sneeringly referred to by the rest of the circuit as 'Leeds Locals'.

Ernest Ould was the son of a local bookmaker and had been a solicitor. None of this commended itself to the Old Etonians and Harrovians and the other snobs on our circuit. He was later made a County Court judge, and standing by the fire in the Robing Room in Leeds I heard the comment of the then leader of the North Eastern Circuit, Raymond Hinchcliffe QC, when he heard of the appointment:

'Disgusting! Not fit to be made a judge! Why, he buys his shirts ready-made at Austin Reed.'

The remark, I am sure, was partially directed at me, since Hinchcliffe well knew that I was in Ernest's chambers in Leeds. In Hinchcliffe's view, and in the view of many others on the circuit, the principal qualification for the exercise of judicial office was having shirts made to measure in Jermyn Street.

It was with that remark that I began to appreciate how unfit I was for judicial office. I bought my shirts at Marks & Spencer.

*

The barrister to whom I became pupil, Rudolph Lyons, later Sir Rudolph, the retired Stipendiary Recorder of Birmingham, who sadly died this year, was a Jew. At the time I joined chambers there was intense anti-semitism and other discrimination both in Leeds and on the North Eastern Circuit. Jews were not allowed to join the Alwoodley or Moortown Golf Clubs. So they built their own, Moorallerton. They were not allowed to join the local Masonic lodges. So they formed their own. Rudolph became a member and wanted me to join, so that it would not be exclusively Jewish. There were few things I would not have done for him, for he was a kindly helpful master in law and a good friend, but joining the Freemasons was one.

Rudolph was the son of one of two Jewish brothers, both tailors, who fled from pogroms in Middle Europe at the turn of the century and arrived penniless in Leeds. Three of the sons were knighted – as Sir Bernard, Sir Jack and Sir Rudolph Lyons – which says something about Jewish tenacity, and perhaps something about English society. Jack has since blotted his copy-book, with his conduct in the Guinness affair, and was lucky not to be sent to prison, but there was a time when he could host a party of 50 millionaires to meet Margaret Thatcher. I prefer to remember him when we were all much younger, and he and his beautiful wife, a Canadian-born pianist, used to entertain me on a Friday night at the ritual Jewish dinner in their house in Alwoodley Lane, which was habitually referred to by the anti-semites of Leeds as 'All-Yid-ly'.

If merit had anything to do with it, Rudolph would have been in the House of Lords, for he was not only a brilliant advocate but also a good lawyer. But there has always been an unofficial quota for Jews on the High Court Bench, the Court of Appeal and the House of Lords. As Lord Hailsham once said, over lunch in the Crypt Restaurant in what are humorously referred to as 'The Royal Courts of Justice' in the Strand: 'If there were not this quota, and it went on talent, the whole judiciary would be Jewish.'

Both Ould and Lyons excelled as advocates. As the Rev. Charles Cabet Colton wrote in *Lacon* in 1820, 'If you want enemies excel others; if you want friends let others excel you.'

*

The art of advocacy is a strange one. It is akin to acting but with the actor having to make up the lines as he goes along. It requires some measure of eloquence, but it is far from the glib flow of words without any discernible meaning which characterises 'Thought for the Day' on Radio 4's 'Today' programme. It must be reasoned, and rational, and persuasive.

There is a great deal of difference between judge advocacy and jury advocacy. The clever advocate before a judge alone hints at, but does not assert positively, the conclusions he wishes the judge to reach, leaving him to think he was clever enough to find them for himself.

With juries it is quite different. As an American poet has said, 'Jurors are there to decide which party has the better advocate.' Conclusions have not merely to be rammed home, but rammed home at least three times, if possible in different words. Not only their reason, but also their prejudices and emotions, have to be stirred. A good advocate is one who can think quickly on his feet and has a real grasp of psychology, so that he can decide in seconds how to treat a witness he has never seen before in his life. Like Trollope's self-made Attorney General in *The Warden*, he has to be 'as bright as a diamond, as cutting and as unimpressionable'.

Ernest Ould and Rudolph Lyons were both superb advocates. Ernest had another quality: he was persistent to the end. He never gave up. In one fought divorce case in which I was against him, I had the judge running all the way with me throughout the case. But Ernest turned the judge's mind right round in his twenty-minute speech at the end of the case. And Rudolph had one talent I conspicuously lacked: numeracy. He could do complicated mental arithmetic in a flash, standing on his feet.

Many, if not most, members of the Bar lack the real talents of advocacy but still make a good living. John Randolph, who was called the same day I was by Gray's Inn – a very nice man who was in chambers next door at No. 39 – once told his clerk that he had never won a case against me in his life and felt defeated even before he started. His clerk, in the mafia of barristers' clerks, told my clerk, who repeated it to me. There did come one day when John felt confident that he would win. It was a civil action for damages for three sheep killed by an Alsatian owned by my client. My client had been convicted by magistrates of possessing a dangerous dog and fined, and the dog had been put down. At the end of his case before Judge Wrangham I didn't get up but said to John: 'Are you sure that's your case and that's all the evidence you wish to adduce?' He said, 'Yes', so I got up and made a submission that there was no case for my client to answer. Wrangham upheld it and dismissed the proceedings. John had failed to adduce evidence that my client owned the dog. He knew he did, I knew he did, but he did not prove it in Court. But John had a good practice and ultimately became Stipendiary Magistrate in Leeds.

A conspicuous case of a lawyer who had no talent for advocacy but prospered was Lord Hailsham, because of his connections and antecedents. He could make a rousing speech to the Tory faithful in conference, but in court he was bumbling, incompetent, pompous, arrogant and full of his own self-importance. What is more, when he lost a case he lost his temper. He was brought up, at vast expense, to appear against me in a defended divorce case in Leeds. When he lost, he turned round in fury to his solicitor and said before the judge had left the bench: 'The man's a bloody fool. Enter an appeal.' The solicitor had more sense than to squander even more of his client's money.

There are other barristers who, after a brief trial at the Bar, realise they haven't the talent to become even run-of-the-mill counsel. These take to politics: hence Tony Barber, Edward Heath and Margaret Thatcher. How much better Britain would be today, if all had been successful advocates.

*

My admission to chambers did little to commend them to the rest of the North Eastern Circuit. For a long time I had been a freelance journalist, and the year before I was called I had started a monthly magazine called *Yorkshire Illustrated*, which still exists as *Yorkshire Life*. It was the first of the county magazines, and although my secretary dismissed it as 'all history and geography' it covered every aspect of Yorkshire and Yorkshiremen from fox-hunting through cricket, of course, to Rugby League football. Almost all the journalists in Leeds contributed to it and I knew them all and was friendly with them.

I continued to edit *Yorkshire Illustrated* for a couple of years after I started practising at the Bar until I became too busy and it was sold off.

The North Eastern Circuit was deeply suspicious of my contacts with journalists and thought that I used them to publicise myself. To *consent* to appear in the public prints was tantamount to advertising, then anathema at the Bar, though blatantly indulged in by its leaders.

So, shortly after I had joined the circuit I was arraigned before the Grand Court of the North Eastern Circuit on a charge of unprofessional conduct in allowing a photograph of myself to appear, with a paragraph, in the *Bradford Telegraph and Argus* a year before I started practising. The day after I was called, Martin Ambery Smith, then a dental student at Leeds and now a retired dental surgeon and, I'm happy to say, still a close friend of mine, took a photograph of me. Unknown to me he gave a copy of it to a friend of his on the Bradford paper.

What the circuit did not know was that my journalism, far from being an asset to my career at the Bar, was a detriment. The *Yorkshire Post* was edited by Arthur Mann, a learned and sober editor. It was a Conservative newspaper, though with great respect for truth and impartiality. The same company also owned the *Leeds Mercury*, edited by Linton Andrews. One day Arthur Mann arrived at his desk to find a note of dismissal. He was to be replaced by Linton Andrews, and the two papers were to be merged. The government of the day thought so poorly of this that they immediately knighted Arthur Mann.

I also thought poorly of it. At the time I was editor of *The Gryphon*, the magazine of Leeds University, and I commented on it adversely in such terms that Linton Andrews sent a furious complaint to the Vice-Chancellor. I was invited to see the Vice-Chancellor and, although I was not actually rebuked, I was gently reminded that the *Yorkshire Post* gave substantial support to the University. This did not please Linton Andrews who gave instructions to all the staff of Yorkshire Conservative Newspapers Ltd, including those on the evening paper, that I was not to be reported, except unfavourably. Therefore in the evening paper reports of cases in which I was involved the words used were often 'Counsel for the defence said'. On one occasion I was rebuked by a High Court judge for some stand I had taken, and so was Henry Scott, son of Paley Scott QC, the Recorder of Leeds, in another court. Every word of my rebuke was published in the *Yorkshire Evening Post*. Not a word of Henry's rebuke appeared. All this was well known to my friends on the paper and was the subject of some amusement.

Linton Andrews, who had turned the staid *Yorkshire Post* into a cheap Tory propaganda rag, had another reason for banning me. Soon after coming to the Bar, I had been selected as Labour candidate for Harrogate. The day Labour wins Harrogate will be the day when the Conservative Party has finally been cremated. I took on the job in the hope that, by fighting a vigorous campaign, I would pin down the Young Conservatives so that they could not spend their time helping in the marginal constituencies of Leeds. Andrews had a strict policy that no publicity of any kind should be given to any Labour candidates.

He also had his revenge on me for the comments I had passed on him in *The Gryphon*. The *Yorkshire Post* was the only newspaper to carry a false report of what I had said about Lord Goddard, the Lord Chief Justice, in the course of a political meeting in Bradford (see Chapter 10 below).

*

Although in 1952, as Christmas Humphreys was ready to point out, I was a comparative novice at the Bar, I had by then already appeared for the defence in four murder cases.

In my first year, 1947, for the autumn assize in Leeds, I was given a brief, neatly tied with red ribbon, which was endorsed on the backsheet with the words:

Brief for the Prisoner
Mr E John Parris

with you

Mr Ralph Cleworth, K.C.
Poor Prisoners' Defence Act

The last line meant that for my labours I would receive the sum of £3 3s out of public funds.

It so happened that at that assize I found myself appearing in not one but two murder trials. In the other case, the junior counsel actually instructed found himself engaged in another court when the case was called on. So I was told by our clerk to 'sit in' for him; that meant that I did the work but did not receive the fee. To some people, unfamiliar with the practice of our courts, it may be surprising that the counsel instructed in a case sometimes never appears. Some accused certainly complain. However, while three, and sometimes four, courts are sitting in the same building it is almost impossible to avoid clashes, at least so long as the rule is maintained that, whatever happens, not one minute of any judge's time must be unoccupied.

By coincidence both these cases concerned crimes committed in or near Doncaster, both the accused were young ex-servicemen, and the same defence was raised in each case. In both cases I had the same leader, and in neither of them did he or I see the accused before the trial. For, as he explained to me as we stood by the fireplace in the robing room waiting for the first case to start, his view was that 'Defending counsel in a murder trial should never have a conference with the accused. Otherwise, counsel's emotions become entangled with those of the prisoner and he is less able to concentrate on the job.'

The other two cases were the defence of the same man, Anthony O'Rourke, for two separate alleged murders. In the first case he had killed an old man. At that trial he was acquitted on a story of self-defence. In the second he had killed an old woman. In that case he was convicted of manslaughter and sentenced to ten years' imprisonment. Since his release he has committed a third murder and is now back in prison with a life sentence.

*

It so happened that I did find out how I had come to be briefed in the Craig and Bentley case.

On 2 November 1952 Christopher Craig's elder brother,

Niven, was already in prison. There another prisoner strongly recommended me to him. Apparently I had once defended this man at Leeds Assize, when he had been acquitted by the jury. He thought this quite an achievement. He had skipped his bail, so that he was not tried when two of his partners in crime were. Both were convicted. Later, on exactly the same evidence on which they had been convicted, I had secured his acquittal. Later still he had been convicted in London of some other crime. (Much of the work of defending counsel consists in getting villains acquitted to continue in their villainy.) Anyway, there is nothing like word-of-mouth recommendation and he had passed it on to Niven Craig, who had passed it on to his parents, who had asked the solicitor for Christopher Craig to instruct me.

*

In those days I was foolish enough still to have my telephone number in the directory. I removed it after I had a call at three in the morning from Tony Waite, the Vicar of St George's Leeds, to ask whether I would appear for the defence of his curate who had just been charged by the police with gross indecency in a public urinal. Without fee of course. I did, but Tony Waite was a former solicitor and should have known better.

It was later one night that I had a call from Harry Proctor, the crime reporter of the *Sunday Pictorial* (now the *Sunday Mirror*). He was well known to me because not only had he been a Leeds journalist, but I had already defended him twice, successfully, in drunk-in-charge cases in Yorkshire.

Harry sounded as if he was ready for another charge of drunken driving if he was driving home to Beckenham. 'We've bought the Craig family,' he slurped triumphantly. 'Madeline and I are going to manage them.'

That was a reference to Madeleine McLoughlin, whom Harry always insisted on calling Madeline.

As I understood it, Harry told me that they had paid the Craig parents £500. Perhaps I am wrong about that, because the Craig parents later claimed they had been paid £350. The difference may well be what the paper paid out to Harry and what the

Craigs got. Receipts weren't given for that sort of business in those days.

It soon became apparent why he had phoned me.

'Will you take me into Brixton Prison when you go to see Craig, so that I can interview him?' he asked. 'You can always tell them I'm your clerk.'

3

Behind the Scenes

'Not bloody likely,' I told Harry Proctor.

Not that that deterred him. I subsequently learned that he got into Brixton Prison on two occasions and interviewed Craig. The story was spread across several issues of the paper as 'My story by Christopher Craig'. Most of it came out of the imagination of Harry Proctor. It could have seriously prejudiced the defence of Craig. However, it was platitudinous and innocuous rubbish.

*

Harry Proctor was an exponent of the journalistic principle 'Make it fast, make it up'.

During the war, he was sent by the *Daily Mail* to write about Dover, as 'the front line town' when it was being heavily bombed. He phoned his story through, as always, just in time for the first edition, and later that evening his editor found him drinking brandy in El Vino in Fleet Street.

'That was a wonderful story you sent in, Harry,' he said. Then the penny dropped. He gasped: 'You sod! You've never been there! You couldn't be back here by now.' Harry, incidentally, was later barred from El Vino.

There was extensive flooding on the East Anglian coast in 1953. By then, Harry was on the staff of the *Sunday Pictorial*, and that paper came out with a front page picture and heart-rending story, written by him, about a babe in a Moses basket which had been found floating in the waters. What the readers were not told was that the photograph was taken miles from the floods: in fact on the Thames in the mud flats which emerge at low tide just below Blackfriars Bridge. Where Harry got the baby from is unknown. It may well have been one of Harry's own, by his patient, long-suffering wife Doreen, by whom he had numerous children, or it may have been one of his equally numerous bastards. Harry was a Christian Scientist Sunday School teacher who succeeded in getting one of his pupils, a fourteen-year-old, pregnant.

Harry had started life as a greengrocer's errand boy in Leeds. He had learnt shorthand and typing in evening class and found himself a job as a messenger on the *Yorkshire Evening Post*. He started contributing news items and eventually got himself accepted as a reporter. Later he graduated to being a crime reporter on the *Daily Mail*.

One of his great scoops on that paper was when he was sent to cover a case, Hulton and Jones, in which an English girl had been involved with an American serviceman in the murder of a taxi driver.

He joined the pack of hacks boozing in the local near the girl's home but later gave them the slip and went to the house. The door was opened by a young sister.

'I'm from Scotland Yard,' announced Harry. 'I wonder did your sister keep a diary which might be of help to her?'

'Yes, she did,' said the sister. 'I'll get it for you.'

Harry took it off.

Some time later he was in the pub boozing with the rest, when the superintendent in charge of the case came in.

'Come on, Proctor, we've got you now,' he said. 'You've been posing as an officer from Scotland Yard.'

'Far from it,' said the innocent-eyed Harry. 'I said I'd come straight from Scotland Yard Press Bureau which is absolutely true. You can check if you like.'

'OK, where's the diary you got from this young bird?'

Harry glanced at his watch. 'It should be with Scotland Yard by now.'

He had sent it by express messenger to his office in London and told them to photocopy it and send it round to Scotland Yard.

Hulton and Jones were convicted and hanged. The newspaper was able to print a reproduction of the diary – which consisted mainly of a list of men with whom the girl had had intercourse. It read like the nominal roll of the United States Army.

*

It may be easy to condemn Harry and his like, but on one occasion at least he served the public interest.

While on the *Mail*, in a way that journalists of today would not dream of doing, he made 'the calls' as he had learnt to do on the local paper. One of these was to the morgues of London. Visiting one, he was shown the body of a newly born child which he was told by the mortuary attendant had been taken out of the Thames.

'Just another of the poor unwanted kids dumped in the river,' the attendant told him.

But Harry was observant. He saw there was a piece of sticking plaster on the child's arm. With his immense experience of childbirth he knew that that meant that the child had been born in a hospital. Persistent, he rang every maternity hospital in London to check whether a child of that age had been born. He drew a blank. Then he started to ring the London General Hospitals and eventually came up with the news that at St Thomas's a child had been born there to a young woman. He got the address and went and spoke to the girl's mother.

'No, my daughter hasn't had a baby,' she told him. 'But she's been in Guy's for the removal of an internal growth. That's what my husband and daughter told me.'

Harry quickly concluded, first, that the father of the child was the girl's father; secondly, that he had collected the baby; and thirdly, that he had got rid of it by dumping it from a bridge over the Thames.

Harry wrote a story to this effect which, incredibly, got past the libel readers and appeared in the *Mail*. Shortly afterwards he was called into a conference with the the editor and managing director and told he was sacked. The *Mail* had received a libel writ and was proposing to publish an apology and pay substantial damages.

As he was leaving the room, Harry turned round to the assembled big-wigs and said:

'If you do this, you'll look a stupid load of fucking cunts, when he's charged with murder.'

'What do you mean?' said the editor.

'He's certain to be charged.'

Instead of being fired, Harry was suspended on full pay for six weeks. On the last Friday of the six weeks the man was arrested for murder, and subsequently he was tried and hanged.

Later Harry met the daughter in a pub. She smashed a glass and jabbed it in his face and accused him of having killed her father. He had indeed. The crime would have gone undetected but for him.

*

Mr and Mrs Craig, having been bought by the *Sunday Pictorial*, were removed from the rest of the press, with their attractive daughter Lucy, to the seclusion and comfort of the Angel Hotel, Shepperton.

A film actor called Alan Ladd was staying there at the time, and Mrs Craig asked for his autograph.

*

The evening after their son was convicted of the murder of a police officer, Harry and Madeleine took the Craig family to dinner at the first-floor restaurant of The Prospect of Whitby, an inn beside the River Thames. There they enjoyed a good dinner with champagne. A speculative photographer came round and took a flash picture of the cheerful party, with Harry standing up with a foaming glass of champagne in his hand toasting the family. Happily for Harry the photographer did not recognise any of them, or he would have been off to Fleet Street to sell it for £1,000. Harry recognised the potential danger, and the surprised photographer was glad to surrender his film to Harry for £100 in cash. He had it developed and when shortly afterwards I was defending him for the third time in a drunk-in-charge case he showed it to me.

The party retreated to the Angel Hotel in Shepperton. Later that night Harry was with Lucy Craig when her father hammered on the door, having been disturbed by noises emanating from his daughter's room. Harry escaped to his own room by creeping on an outside ledge.

Harry had still to produce in time for the first edition of the *Sunday Pictorial* an 'exclusive' story. He had already written it. It was on the theme 'How I failed my son' by Captain Niven Craig. What is more, the news editor, Fred Redman, knowing Harry, had insisted that not only should Mr Craig sign it but he should sign every page of it.

But Mr Craig did not think that he had failed his son. In his view he had behaved like any other responsible parent and other factors were the cause of the delinquencies of his two sons. It took Harry more than one bottle of Scotch to persuade him to put his initials on every page and to sign Harry's work of fiction. It was just in time. Harry was able to telephone it through triumphantly to the copytaker for the first editions. It made the main lead story on front and back pages.

EXCLUSIVE: A TERRIBLE WARNING TO PARENTS.
MY FAILURE: BY CRAIG'S FATHER.

According to that article he was to be condemned because, 'by lavishing love upon this youngster and by believing all the rot preached about full freedom for young children', he was more responsible for 'the state of affairs than the young thugs themselves'. The article went on: 'I scarcely ever in the whole of my life raised a hand to Chris. Now I wish I had given him a damn good hiding years ago ....'

These, of course, were not the sentiments of Mr Craig. Nor were they, I believe, the sentiments of Harry Proctor who, I am sure, never raised a hand to any of his children, however drunk he was. But it was what the readers of the *Sunday Pictorial* wanted to read, so he gave it to them.

Scapegoat

*

Harry Proctor and the *Sunday Pictorial* lost all interest in Christopher Craig after his conviction. Harry then managed to ingratiate himself with the Bentley family and to buy their story. As a result, the *Pictorial* was able to publish exclusively the last letter Bentley wrote to his parents before his execution:

> Oh Dad! Don't let my cycle frames get rusty they might come in handy one day 'cos old Sally has got a cracked frame and I want you to change it before something happens to you, and Dad, keep a strict eye on Denis if he does anything wrong, though I don't think he will but you never know how little things can get you into trouble, if he does, wallop him so that he won't be able to sit for three weeks. I am trying to give you good advice because of my experience.
>
> I tell you what Mum, the truth of this story has got to come out one day, and as I said in the visiting box that one day a lot of people are going to get into trouble and I think you know who those people are ....

Since Bentley could not write, the letter was said to have been written for him by a warder. It is more likely that it was concocted by Harry Proctor.

*

Lucy Craig, having got married shortly after the trial of her brother for murder, made an application to emigrate to Australia. She must have told Harry, because he went round to Australia House and asked: 'Do you know this girl is the sister of the convicted murderer, Christopher Craig?'

As a result Australia refused her permission to emigrate and Harry got another exclusive story for the *Sunday Pictorial*.

*

Not long after the trial of Craig and Bentley, Harry Proctor was once again indicted for driving a car under the influence of drink. Not having paid my fees for previous defences, he was reluctant to engage me again and his solicitors instructed a counsel called Dunlop. Dunlop, however, advised that the evidence against Harry was so damning that he should plead guilty. Harry, according to the police, had been chased all round the Elephant & Castle roundabout (in those days it had no traffic lights) and stopped further down the road. As usual, his car was littered with half-empty half-bottles of brandy and he stank of drink.

Harry refused to accept the advice of his counsel, dismissed him and opted for me. The trial took place in London in a court which had been converted from a swimming bath. Harry was in the dock, and adjacent to it was the jury room, with only thin plaster-board walls. When it was announced that the jury had reached a verdict, I returned to court. As I came in, Harry in the dock, looking jubilant, gave me a thumbs-up signal.

He was acquitted.

When I met Dunlop later, he said: 'I hear you fucked up the coppers properly.'

I had indeed.

*

Harry was soon on trial yet again for the same offence. This time he was driving up the A1 to go and see his daughter, who was a reporter on the Doncaster edition of the *Evening Post*. He stopped on the way at a fish-and-chip shop. There was a queue to be served and he turned to the man behind him and said:

'Will you keep my place in the queue? I'm pissed as a newt and want to put my car round the back so that the coppers don't knock me off.'

The man said: 'I'm afraid you're dead unluckly. I'm a police officer and I'm arresting you on your own admission for driving under the influence.'

This time Harry, who had not paid any of my fees for the previous three cases, did not have the face to instruct me again. I was told later that he was sent to prison for three months, during which time he organised the prisoners into making wooden toys for children at Christmas which he sold to his immense profit. But that may have been mere gossip.

I never did get paid for the three cases in which I defended Harry Proctor. In theory a solicitor is responsible for the payment of fees to counsel. When, after I had left the Bar, I complained to the Law Society that the solicitor had not paid my fees, I received the reply that the solicitor had not been paid by his client. That, in their view, was an adequate defence. It was perfectly true. But the solicitor in all three cases had taken out second mortgages over Harry's house to cover both his charges and my fees.

Harry was, I believe, eventually sacked by the *Sunday Pictorial* for stealing from his colleagues. He later wrote a book entitled *The Street of Disillusion*. I read the typescript of his first version, which was very interesting. However, it was thoroughly castrated by the publishers' libel lawyers and, among other things, all the flattering references to me as an advocate were deleted. Counsel had apparently advised that it would cause me embarrassment, and the copy which eventually appeared was thoroughly anaemic and uninteresting.

*

While Harry was busy interviewing my client in prison and delighting the readers of the *Pictorial* with his inventions, I was up in Leeds defending a client who was alleged to have received gold stolen from a Sheffield precious metals refinery.

I received my brief from Craig's solicitor, Nelson, on the afternoon of Tuesday, 2 December. Normally, a brief for a defendant contains a summary of the case against the accused with his answer to all the points; a statement of the evidence he will give to the court, and the depositions: that is the evidence given on oath in the magistrates' court by the witnesses for the prosecution. In 1952 it was not the practice for the Director of Public Prosecutions to supply counsel for the defence in murder trials with all the statements taken by the police from witnesses. My brief for Craig consisted of nothing more than the depositions and the brief sentence:

Counsel will obtain all the information he needs from the

depositions enclosed herewith and conference with his client.

That evening, I arranged to leave my junior, Helen Paling (now a Circuit Judge), on the case and chartered a plane to take me down from Leeds/Bradford Airport to London to see Lord Goddard, the Lord Chief Justice, who was to preside over the case.

My brief had been delivered on Tuesday, 2 December. The trial before Lord Goddard was to take place at the Old Bailey on Thursday, 4 December. There was no way in which I could abandon my clients at the Leeds Assize to appear in London on 4 December. Still less could I, or indeed any other counsel, see Craig and appear fully briefed by Thursday. I therefore chartered the plane at my own expense. The trip by air wasn't an enormous success. The plane was ordered to land at Hendon Airport, from where a hired car took some 40 minutes to get me to the Old Bailey. However, I was in time to see Lord Goddard in his room there, with Christmas Humphreys, counsel for the Crown, and Frank Cassels, counsel for Derek Bentley.

Lord Goddard did not welcome my application to have the case adjourned for a week.

4

Lord Goddard

In fact, Lord Goddard was positively hostile, and at first he
categorically refused to grant me an adjournment.

I pointed out that I had only received the brief the previous
day and that I was engaged in a long trial at Leeds Assize.

'You can return the brief. There are plenty of other counsel
available in London,' he told me.

I opened the brief and showed him my instructions.

'Even if I were to return it now,' I said, 'it would be impossible
for any counsel to be ready for trial tomorrow.'

Even this didn't impress him.

'Well, he's got no defence. He's going to plead guilty, isn't he?'

'I don't know that until I've seen him.'

'Well, he's got no defence.'

'He may well have. If he was not shooting at the officers, he
may be guilty only of manslaughter.'

I had derived this idea from reading the depositions.
According to Fairfax, he had been only a few feet from Craig
when the youth fired directly at him. Yet the bullet which struck
him had ripped a hole in his jacket, rolled over his shoulder and
was later found near his braces at his back. When I read that, I
phoned my wife's cousin, Major Chivers of the Wiltshire
Regiment, who was a ballistics expert. He confirmed what I had
myself thought probable. No shot fired at that range from a .455
Eley revolver could possibly have done so little damage. It was
obviously a spent bullet, a ricochet from the ground or some
other hard surface, and not aimed at the officer.

'Rubbish,' said Goddard. 'A police officer has been murdered.'

'It might have been accidental.'

'That's no defence. If a police officer is killed while in the course of arresting a criminal, it matters not that the act that killed him was deliberate or accidental. That's the law and has been for centuries.'

'I'm afraid I don't agree.'

Goddard snorted with contempt. 'You'd better go and look at the cases.'

'I have,' I said.

'Well, you're not getting an adjournment. It would be grossly inconvenient to me, and I expect to the other counsel.'

Humphreys and Cassels nodded.

'Very well, Lord Chief,' I said. 'As soon as you sit at 10.30 in court, I'm going to make a public application to you for an adjournment. I propose to say to you in public that my client has specifically and particularly asked for me to defend him. I'm going to tell you that I only received the brief yesterday. I'm going to tell you in public the only instructions I have received. I propose to say that, if your Lordship refuses an adjournment, it will be a total denial of justice to a youth accused of murder. I cannot and will not attend to defend my client tomorrow. If he is unrepresented you will be responsible. I think it might attract some attention from the Press.'

Goddard's features, generally a pallid version of a bullfrog's, went purple. He struck out with his fist at me in rage. It stopped a few inches from my nose.

Then, like a deflated balloon, his mood suddenly changed. He went white again and said:

'Very well, you shall have your adjournment to next Tuesday. But I don't propose to leave the issue of murder or manslaughter to the jury.'

But what was more influential in his decision was the fact that I had pointed out to him that if he started the case on Thursday morning I could easily keep it going so that it went into the Monday. And I knew, and he knew, that on the Monday he was due to preside over the Court of Criminal Appeal.

*

4. Lord Goddard

It was not the first confrontation I had had with the Lord Chief Justice. In the winter of 1951 he appeared at Leeds Assize. The list for the first day was filled in the Crown Court with pleas of 'Guilty' with which his Lordship dealt with great dispatch. There was consternation in the cells under the Court as man after man returned there, after a few minutes above, with the sort of sentences which made the waiting crowd below tremble for their fate and provoked the rudest words the English language contains. Even the warders were aghast.

That day I was appearing to mitigate for a thirty-year-old miner who was charged with attempted shopbreaking. At half-past eleven on a Friday night, his pay day, he was seen to throw a brick through a shop window. He obligingly sat on a wall opposite for some time until the police arrived and then ran away. After a short chase he fell down in a garden and was unconscious for twenty minutes. He was very much under the influence of drink even when he came round, and he said to the officers who arrested him: 'I don't think I broke and entered, did I? I don't know owt about it.'

Had that offence stood alone, he might no doubt have been acquitted, for drunkenness could negate the essential elements of *mens rea*. Juries are usually disposed to be fairly generous to men who do things like this when they are drunk and have no real intention of committing crimes of dishonesty. However, while in police custody he confessed that he had done much the same thing to the same shop twice before, also when, as he put it, he was 'stupid drunk'. On one of those occasions he had taken away some tobacco and two pairs of socks. The tobacco he had thrown away in a field, whence it was recovered and returned to the shop, but the socks were never found. He also admitted one other offence: attempting to break-and-enter another shop. All four crimes had been committed on pay day when he had taken a great deal of drink.

Apart from his confession, the police had no reason to suspect that he was the culprit, and they had no evidence whatever against him.

The accused pleaded guilty to all the charges. Unfortunately, he had been convicted before for similar offences and had been sentenced to six months in 1946 and nine months in 1947. Two of the collieries where he had been employed described him as a good worker and regular attender, but the colliery where he was then employed said he was a poor worker and an irregular attender. His average wages were £10 a week.

In the middle of my cross-examination of the police officer who was giving this information Lord Goddard suddenly asked:

'I suppose drink is this man's trouble, is it not?'

'It is, my Lord,' replied the officer.

I asked the officer: 'Does he suffer from gastritis?'

'I do not know about that.'

'He has to go for an X-ray?'

'Yes.'

The Lord Chief Justice said: 'He got off lightly in 1946; only eighteen months in 1947; and now he breaks out again. I do not want to deprive the country of a coal getter.' (In fact it was only nine months he got in 1947.) He then asked the police officer whether the colliery wanted him back.

'Yes, my Lord,' said the officer.

'Although he is a poor workman and irregular attender?'

'Yes, the employment is still open for him.'

'They will take anybody, I suppose.'

I tried to chip in: 'There is an explanation of his irregular attendance that he has given me. He suffers from gastritis.'

The Lord Chief Justice: 'That is caused by drink, I suppose?'

I said: 'Nobody can say that until the 15th of November, when he is X-rayed. He has a note in his pocket at the moment, which I have seen, instructing him to appear at hospital for X-ray and treatment.'

'I want to know when he is going back to work,' said the Lord Chief.

I asked the police officer: 'He was working at the time, was he not?'

'Yes.'

'What about his health?' said the Lord Chief. 'I might take a particular course in this case, that of making it very difficult for him to get any drink by a fine. If I dealt with it in that way that would take most of his money, so that he does not drink. Is he on bail with sureties?'

'Yes, one surety – his mother.'

'I think I had better wait and hear what the report on him is. I shall be here on the 16th or 17th if necessary.'

Lord Goddard then addressed the accused in the most jovial manner.

'I will enlarge your bail, so you can go to hospital. You have to come back here on the day after you have been to hospital. In any case, you have got to be here first thing in the morning, by half-past ten on the morning of the 16th. That is tomorrow week. Do you understand?'

'Yes, my Lord.'

'You come back and I will see what the doctors say about you. You had better ask the doctors to give you a chit, or whatever they call it.'

'Thank you, my Lord.'

As the prisoner was leaving the dock, Lord Goddard added, even more genially: 'Mind you, I've not decided what I'm going to do with you.'

The accused came out of the dock in somewhat elated and relieved. There was little doubt in his mind, in spite of the Lord Chief's cautionary rider, that if he were fit to continue his work he would be fined and not sent to prison. His solicitor and I thought so too, because it was wholly exceptional for any man who had pleaded guilty to felony to be allowed out on bail.

We were in for a rude awakening.

On 16 November the case was duly called on and the prisoner appeared in the dock.

I rose to my feet: 'May it please you, my Lord, I appear for the defendant. Your Lordship put the case back because he was due for a medical examination yesterday. Your Lordship took the view that, as he was a miner and the source of his trouble has been drinking, the course of justice might be met by fining him, if he could continue work.'

I thought, as I still think, that it was a fair summary of the previous hearing. Lord Goddard took a different view, and there was no geniality about the way he said: 'I did not say that. I certainly did not.' He then asked a question which to my mind

41

indicated that he had forgotten completely about the previous proceedings: 'Do you say that he was due for a medical examination? Was it for the Army?'

'No. It is a case where his own doctor sent him for an examination. I will hand your Lordship the information, if you desire it.'

I put in the medical certificate. Lord Goddard glanced at it and then picked up the papers on the case. He read out the offences and said to the accused:

'There is no question about it that I dare say that drink is the bottom of your trouble; but you are one of those men that in drink are making a nuisance to the community.'

He picked up and read out the accused's list of previous convictions. 'Now you are up before me for four cases. I cannot pass it over. You must go to prison for two years.'

This *volte-face* left me seething with indignation. For one thing I had been afforded no opportunity to make a speech in mitigation of the offence. For another, it seemed to me quite wrong that a man should have held out to him the prospect of his liberty, only to have it snatched from him at the last moment. It was cat-and-mouse treatment. Justice, I thought, perhaps quite wrongly, had not been 'seen to have been done'.

The difficulty was that, on the face of it, it was not an entirely unreasonable sentence. The grounds of appeal made clear our real objection to it. I was therefore surprised to find when I arrived in the Court of Criminal Appeal that the tribunal was being presided over by Lord Goddard himself.

I expressed my dissatisfaction that he should be sitting on the case.

'This Court has repeatedly said that it is often desirable to have the trial judge sitting,' he told me.

I said that, in view of what I would have to say, I could hardly believe that it would be advantageous in the present case either to the Court or the appellant.

'Very well, Mr Parris,' said Lord Goddard. 'You shall have a special Court of Criminal Appeal for you tomorrow morning at ten o'clock.'

Nothing could have suited my own convenience less. It meant two days spent in London right in the middle of an Assize.

4. Lord Goddard

My special Court of Criminal Appeal listened to me in silence and refused leave to appeal.

'We have had the advantage of discussing this matter with Lord Goddard,' said Mr Justice Hilbery, presiding, 'and he tells us that he remembered perfectly all about the case. As for the point that counsel was given no opportunity to make a speech in mitigation, we consider that there is no substance in this complaint. I have never known a mitigation which affected my mind.'

*

Rayner Goddard was born in 1877. According to his obsequious biographer, Fenton Bresler, he came of stock 'as English as ancient oak'. They were descended, he claimed, from Norsemen who believed that the origination of their race was one Odin, a god king and the name Goddard originated with Godord, meaning priest king. The family, it is said, continued as land owners around Swindon into the nineteenth century and rely upon passages in a work by Richard Jefferies, author of that most wonderful book about boyhood, *Bevis*. This was entitled *The Goddards of North Wilts*, in which he asserts 'the history of Swindon, since it became a place, is, in fact, the history of the family of Goddard'.

The truth is that Rayner Goddard had no connection whatsoever with the great family of Goddards of Swindon. One account is that his grandfather was a Jewish refugee named Gottlieb who became a successful speculative builder in Lewisham, converted and changed his name to Goddard. His father, Charles Goddard, born in 1842, became a solicitor and, with a partnership in a London firm, was able to send his son to Marlborough. Two of his fellow pupils were known to me. Both of them describe him as a notorious bully of smaller boys and one whose favourite entertainment for his dormitory was to recite the death sentence. From Marlborough he went to Oxford. He had difficulty in being called to the Bar because Roman law was an essential subject in those days and he failed the examination five times. He managed to pass on his sixth attempt – his last chance.

Lord Goddard has told how his career at the Bar began with

what he termed 'one of those strokes of luck which I firmly believe play a big part in human affairs'. Sitting in Chambers one day without work of any kind to do, he began opening and shutting drawers aimlessly. In one, he discovered an old law report and, glancing through it casually, he came upon a case which dealt with banking and explained how the clearing houses operate. The next day, a Saturday, he was alone in Chambers when some men arrived with a brief. They had already tried three other sets of chambers without finding any counsel in. They were solicitors from the Midland Bank, and they asked him a question which had been decided by the very case he had read the day before. He was able to answer it without difficulty. He got the brief and a regular client. Soon other banks were coming to him as well. Yet until he had read that old case he confesses that he knew practically nothing about banking at all.

After three recorderships, which were then entirely part-time jobs, he was appointed to the High Court Bench in 1932. He served under Lord Hewart, described by David Napley in *Murder at the Villa Madeira* as 'one of the least satisfactory of the Lords Chief Justice of England – rude, arrogant, disputatious and with little of the milk of human kindness'. He served in the Criminal Justice Appeal Court until 1946, when he was appointed Lord Chief Justice by Clement Attlee at the age of 69. It was a bizarre appointment for a Labour Prime Minister to make, especially since Attlee did not know Goddard and appointed him without consulting his own Lord Chancellor, Earl Jowitt.

*

In theory judges are appointed by the monarch on the advice of the Lord Chancellor. In practice they are appointed by the Prime Minister of the day. But by a convention which went back to the seventeenth century the office of Lord Chief Justice of England was regarded as the perquisite of the Attorney-General in office when the post fell vacant.

The one exception was that of Hewart, who did a deal with the Prime Minister, Lloyd George, that there would be a stop-gap

Lord Chief Justice until he was ready to take the post. Therefore Mr Justice A.T. Lawrence became Lord Chief Justice of England, with the title of Lord Trevethin. His chief virtue was that he was 75 years old on appointment. When Hewart was ready to take the job, Trevethin was pushed out. He first learned that he had resigned when he read it in *The Times*.

The Lord Chancellor at the time of Goddard's appointment, Earl Jowitt, told me categorically that it was in fact Labour's Attorney-General, Hartley Shawcross, who recommended Attlee to appoint Goddard and that he had not been consulted in any way. Later I wrote to Attlee to check this. He did not deny it, but thought it unlikely that he had not consulted Jowitt. 'If I had neglected to consult him, he would not have been slow to protest.' However, Jowitt was in India at the time that Goddard's appointment was announced, and I think he was telling the truth.

In 1946 when Goddard got the job, Hartley Shawcross, the Attorney-General, was only 44. He entertained high hopes of succeeding Attlee as leader of the Labour Party and Prime Minister. Attlee at the time was already 63 and obviously was not going to lead the Party for very long. In fact he continued for only nine more years.

According to Shawcross, Attlee did offer him the job, but only in a negative way: 'I don't suppose you want it.'

In getting Attlee to appoint the 69-year-old Goddard I think Shawcross was keeping his options open. If he didn't become leader of the Labour Party and Prime Minister or Lord Chancellor, he could later exercise his right, as Hewart had done with Trevethin, to the office of Lord Chief Justice.

In fact in 1953, when he was 76, Lord Goddard contemplated retirement as Lord Chief Justice. According to Lord Parker of Waddington, who was eventually to succeed him, he was prepared to go that year if Hartley Shawcross could succeed him. But by then Shawcross was not greatly in favour with his own party (where he was known as 'Sir Shortly Floorcross') or with the Tories. Neither was prepared to see Shawcross as Lord Chief Justice, so Goddard hung on.

The relationship between Goddard and Shawcross was always

a close one. A solicitor told me that he had gone to have a conference with Shawcross at his home on a Saturday afternoon in an important case. The case was to be heard before the Lord Chief Justice the following week.

'Do you think we'll have problems with Goddard?' asked the solicitor.

'I don't think so,' replied Shawcross. 'In fact, he's down there at the moment in the garden.' The solicitor looked out of the French windows and there was the Lord Chief Justice of England weeding Shawcross's garden.

Why did Clem Attlee, undoubtedly the best Prime Minister this country has had this century, appoint somebody who hated the working class and those who represent them, the Labour Party, with every atom of his being?

*

Goddard had been an independent Conservative candidate put up to oppose a barrister, Sir William Davison, the sitting Conservative member for South Kensington in 1929. Sir William had divorced his adulterous wife and Goddard, along with a part of the local Conservative Party, thought this made him unsuitable to represent them in Parliament. At the election Sir William Davison romped home with 28,049 votes and Goddard crept in, bottom of the poll, with 6,365.

His conduct in the libel action that Harold Laski, Professor of Political Science at the London School of Economics, brought against various newspapers in 1946 for alleging that as Chairman of the National Executive of the Labour Party he had advocated revolution by violence was as partisan and as dishonest as that of Lord Hewart in the libel action brought by the pioneer of birth control, Marie Stopes. In his summing up he told the jury that what Harold Laski had said amounted to: 'If the capitalists do not give way, it is the proletariat or working class or labourers, or whatever you like to call it, who will use violence for the purpose of getting their way.' He compared this to a man stopping somebody in the street and saying, 'Give me your wallet', and then went on to discuss the conduct of the mobs in the French Revolution. The jurors, who were a 'special jury' consisting of those who held substantial property, needless to say returned a verdict for the defendants.

As Laski wrote, and left unpublished when he died, only three years later (his wife attributed his death to his treatment by Goddard in the action): 'The judge not only hates the opinions you hold, but will explain to the jury that they are dangerous opinions ... What you swiftly see as the real issue at stake is not what was said at some place on a definite occasion, but the fact that you hold unpopular opinions which both judge and jury are convinced it is bad to hold and worse by far to express.'

Later in life, according to his biographer, Goddard laughingly described the jury's verdict as 'a grave miscarriage of justice'. 'This was said with a broad smile, a chuckle and almost a wink.' In other words, he was well aware that he and the special jury had happily conspired to pervert the course of justice. He even described one of the defendant's witnesses as an 'obvious perjurer'. How, then, did Attlee come to appoint this dishonest political fascist to the office of Lord Chief Justice of England?

He told me: 'I knew nothing about Goddard. Shawcross persuaded me that the judiciary had become slack and inefficient. Goddard, he claimed, would discipline them and "tone-up the system".'

Why did Shawcross tell him that? Partly because, incredibly, he was a friend of Goddard's; but, more important, because, as we have seen, he hoped to step into his shoes in due course as Lord Chief Justice of England if he did not achieve his ambition to become Prime Minister.

*

Lord Denning in his introduction to Bresler's biography of Goddard wrote: 'This book tells the story of a great man ...'; 'Rayner Goddard was the very embodiment of the common law'; 'He had a firm grasp of principle. He delighted in legal argument.'

Almost every word of that is completely untrue; and untrue to the certain knowledge of Lord Denning. Goddard, as Denning

47

admits, 'rarely read the papers beforehand'. His knowledge of the law would have disgraced a first-year law student. He ignored precedents, which in theory were legally binding on him. Even if they were his own cases he would dismiss them with 'I must have been wrong then'. Far from being 'the very embodiment of the common law', he neither had a grasp of it nor gave a tuppenny damn for it.

He lacked every judicial quality. He would not listen and made up his mind within minutes without hearing the evidence. (Later I will describe a case when this turned out to my advantage.) After that, nothing would change his mind and he just switched off and didn't listen to the evidence or to argument.

A good judge not only reads the pleadings or depositions in advance but listens patiently to all the evidence and arguments before reaching a conclusion. Goddard was habitually offensive and insulting in public to counsel who appeared before him. The weak he terrorised. Even Lord Denning acknowledges that. 'The formidable Chief Justice put them in fear,' he wrote. Goddard even intimidated other judges. When sitting with others, often he would not consult them but would toss off his judgment. The others would sit there like rabbits paralysed in the headlights of a car, unable to move or utter a word.

At the same time he was at heart a coward. He picked only on those he could browbeat. But those who were prepared to stand up to him and were not afraid of having a row in public with him he left alone. In one criminal case he tried to stop me asking a question of a prosecution witness. I said: 'No doubt if your Lordship thought the answer would be in favour of the prosecution it would be allowed.' It was the most insulting remark that could be made in public to any judge. He capitulated. 'All right – go on – ask it,' he snapped. Thereafter he did not treat me as he did most counsel.

Goddard's worst characteristic as a judge was the way he got through the case lists. He always had more cases put in his list than any judge could possibly cope with, so that counsel and witnesses were left hanging about to meet his pleasure. Jimmy Cassels, father of Frank, was once sitting in the Court of

48

4. Lord Goddard

Criminal Appeal with Goddard. The Lord Chief Justice went through the central door on to the Bench. Mr Justice Cassels had to go through a further door. 'I shall have to hurry,' he said, 'or the case will be on and over before I get there.'

But Goddard's worst feature was his personal character as a man. His daughter, Lady Sachs, wife of Lord Justice Sachs – who was commonly known at the Bar, like a racehorse, as 'Son-in-Law out of Legal Aid' – said of him that he was 'mentally rigorous, contentious, cantankerous, prejudiced, fair-minded, infinitely compassionate and a lovable human being'. Compassionate and lovable he may have been to his family, but on and off the Bench he had no trace of compassion, still less of sensibility. His favourite after-dinner joke was to tell how, at Winchester Assize, he had sentenced three men to be hanged, immediately after which a barrel organ in the street below struck up the Eton Boating song: 'We'll all swing together ... .' He thought it funny.

His clerk, Arthur Smith, told me he used to take a spare pair of striped trousers round for Goddard because he knew that Goddard always had an ejaculation in his pants when sentencing a youth to be flogged or hanged.

Those opposed to capital punishment have said that if the judges had themselves to execute their sentences there would be no convictions. Goddard would have relished the task.

*

Two weapons were used in Britain for inflicting corporal punishment on prisoners. The cat-o'-nine tails had nine lashes of whipcord and could inflict permanent scars. That was referred to as 'flogging'. The other, the birch, was a scarcely less formidable weapon. It had an overall length of 48 inches of birch canes, measured nine inches in circumference and weighed twelve ounces. It was used, after being soaked in water, on a naked body.

'What harm can there be in the birch?' asked a Lord Chief Justice at a meeting of magistrates. The year was 1959, not 1759.

Lord Goddard was an enthusiast for the use of both.

The House of Commons in 1947 passed a Criminal Justice Bill which abolished corporal punishment. By an amendment, moved by Sydney Silverman MP, of which the Government did not approve, it also abolished hanging. Lord Goddard made his maiden speech in the House of Lords in favour of corporal punishment and hanging. The House of Lords returned the Bill to the Commons, and a compromise was arrived at when it returned: corporal punishment was abolished, but hanging was retained. This led Lord Goddard to start a public campaign for the restoration of flogging.

'The Lord Chief Justice has been canvassing for powers to order flogging as enthusiastically as an usher in a Victorian charity school,' commented the then Bishop of Stepney, Dr Joost de Blank (later to become Archbishop of Capetown).

On 25 October 1952 Lord Goddard returned to the battle in the House of Lords. He claimed that he received three or four letters a day from people 'wanting to know what I am going to do to restore flogging'. He used his position on the Bench regularly to lecture about the need for flogging to be reintroduced.

Of Goddard's period in office, Terence Morris in *Crime and Criminal Justice since 1945*, a volume in a series sponsored by the Institute of Contemporary British History, wrote:

> No account of the period of the late 1940s and 1950s could exclude reference to the dominance in the criminal courts of Rayner Goddard. From his appointment until his retirement ... he was an *éminence grise* who overshadowed the whole process of criminal justice.

After quoting David Napley's description of Lord Hewart, he continued:

> Many of those who appeared before Goddard would consider he shared some of those unenviable qualities. On the Bench, he presented a fearsome and positively cadaverous appearance. He did not disguise the fact that he had no sympathy for criminals and certainly none for those who sought to mitigate their crimes by providing social or psychological explanations. He was contemptuous of psychiatrists, social workers and probation officers.

4. Lord Goddard

*

The Saturday before the trial it looked as if I might not get out to Brixton Prison to see my client. The worst smog ever recorded descended upon London. Visibility was reduced to zero. Buses and trams ceased to run, and it is said that 4,000 people died and thousands went to hospital.

I had my car in London but decided it was complete folly to venture out there. So, after much telephoning, I eventually secured a hire car and driver. It took us four hours to get from Westminster to Brixton Prison. The defence of Christopher Craig was turning out to be a very expensive hobby.

5

Christopher Craig

Much of police activity creates crime rather than suppresses it. In one case in which I was involved a habitual burglar was licensed by Leeds Police to commit crimes in Bradford or Hull, or indeed anywhere but on their patch, since he was a paid informer living in the city and enjoyed the confidence of the criminal fraternity. He received strong protection from the Leeds Police when eventually he was arrested by another force.

But quite apart from that, the relentless drive to secure convictions at any cost often makes determined criminals out of those wrongly convicted and their relatives. On Friday 31 October, before the events of that Sunday evening, 2 November, Christopher Craig had seen his elder brother Niven Scott Craig convicted and sentenced to 12 years' imprisonment. In sentencing him, Mr Justice Hilbery had said:

You have, by your record, already shown that you are a young man determined to indulge in desperate crime. I have watched you carefully in the course of this trial and I can say that I do not remember, in the course of some seventeen years on the Bench trying various crimes of violence, a young man of your age who struck me as being so determined as you have impressed me as being.

Now I have heard your record I am confirmed in the view that you are a very exceptionally determined man. You are not only cold-blooded but from my observation of you I have not the least hesitation in saying I believe that you would shoot down, if you had the opportunity to do so, any police officer who was attempting to arrest you or, indeed, any lawful citizen who tried to prevent you from committing some felony which you had in hand.

I think you would do it absolutely coldly, utterly regardless of the pain you might inflict. I am not at all sure that you ought not to have had more than the other men concerned in that robbery, for this reason: I am sure you were the organiser, if not the leader.

I have little doubt it was you who held the gun and that these others were men of rougher material acting under your directions. You will go to prison for twelve years.

Present in Court was the mother of Niven Scott Craig. As her other son, young Christopher Craig, led her sobbing down the steps of the Old Bailey into the street, there were two police officers standing by.

'Well, we've got rid of that bugger for a bit,' one taunted them.

Yet Christopher Craig may have the best of reasons for knowing that Niven had got 12 years in prison for a crime that he did not commit.

*

On 15 March 1952 the occupiers of a house in Honey Lane, Waltham Abbey, a Mr and Mrs Whiten, woke up in the middle of the night to find a torch shining in their faces. A number of masked men, four or five (they were uncertain quite how many), surrounded their bed. The raiders demanded the key of a safe at Mr Whiten's business premises. The did not get it. Both Mr and Mrs Whiten were tied up and searched. The key was not found on either of them and the house was ransacked from top to bottom. It was in fact not in the house, and the robbers departed with no other spoil than £4, a cigarette lighter and a few ball-point pens.

A large American-style car had been seen to arrive at the house. At three o'clock that morning a car of a similar type (though never identified as being the same one), a Buick, was found upside down in a ditch. In the car was a cycle lamp and a hat. About a mile away a man well known to the police, George Albert King, was found on foot. The cycle lamp in the car had his fingerprints on it and the hat was his. That was enough to connect him with the car. The only thing to connect him with the robbery was a Scroll ball-point pen in his pocket – similar to one stolen from Honey Lane. At that time the Scroll company had the exclusive right to manufacture the Biro patented ball-point in the United Kingdom. So if anybody had a ball-point, it would have been a Scroll (the company was later taken over by the United States company of Scripto).

'Ginger' King, as he was known to the police, had another nickname in the underworld. He was known as 'Cat's-eyes' King. Though he suffered from night blindness, so that in the dark he could scarcely see at all, he would drive a car flat out and guide it only by the rumble of the cat's-eyes in the middle of the road. It was, perhaps, the hazards of that form of navigation which crashed the Buick that night. Slender though the evidence was to connect him with the crime at Waltham Abbey, King was convicted and sentenced; but even then he refused to reveal who his associates were. Shortly afterwards he died in prison from tuberculosis, without divulging his secret.

The police began an investigation into the history of the Buick car. They found that it had been bought shortly before by Niven Scott Craig for £200, but it was registered, not in his name, but in that of a man called Cyril Burnley. When the police called at the homes of these men to ask them a few questions both had vanished.

*

It was September before they were traced.

Niven Scott Craig was arrested in a house in Kensington Gardens Square, Paddington. When the police burst into his room he was in bed with a girl-friend called Peggy. According to the police officers, he put his hand under the pillow and tried to pull a gun on them. One leapt on him and wrenched it from his hand. Cyril Burnley was found in another room of the same house, and under his bed was a load of stolen furs.

Both men appeared for trial at the Old Bailey. Niven Scott Craig was charged with armed robbery on 15 March 1952 at the house in Honey Lane, Waltham Abbey, and also with being in possession of an automatic pistol with intent to endanger life. He pleaded not guilty to both offences. Cyril Burnley was also charged with the armed robbery, and with stealing or receiving the furs. He pleaded guilty to receiving the furs knowing them to have been stolen, but denied the armed robbery at Waltham Abbey.

The whole of the evidence for the prosecution against Niven Craig in respect of the Waltham Abbey charge rested on the fact that a car he had bought some weeks before had, by inference, been used for the crime, and that afterwards he had successfully kept out of the way of the police for six months.

He admitted the purchase of the car and said that it had been registered in Burnley's name only because, when it was due to be relicensed, he was ill in bed with flu and could not make the journey to the County Hall to do it himself. On the weekend of the crime he lent the Buick to George King to try out, with a view to purchasing it from him, and himself hired a small car and drove down to Norfolk for a weekend's rabbit shooting.

He called a farmer friend, of impeccable reputation, to give evidence that, at the time the crime was committed, he was in Norfolk, miles away from Waltham Abbey, and could not possibly have taken part in it. He explained his disappearance from his home by saying that he had seen a photograph of the crashed car reproduced in the *Daily Mirror* with the information that the police believed it to be the car used by the bandits. When he saw the car and recognised it, he realised that King must have used the car for the robbery and he was afraid that, with his past record, he would be implicated in the crime. A copy of the newspaper was produced with the photograph, which showed plainly the number.

His defence, therefore, inevitably involved disclosing to the jury that he had previous convictions. Even so, it might well have succeeded had this case been tried alone. The fact that a man's car is used for crime is really quite inadequate proof of an allegation that a man was actually present at the scene, particularly when a witness of perfectly good character vouches for the fact that, at the material time, he was more than a hundred miles away. It was suspicious – but nothing more, and certainly not enough to discharge the burden on the prosecution to satisfy the jury of his guilt beyond reasonable doubt.

However innocent Niven Scott Craig may have been of this crime, he stood no chance at all when the same jury at the same trial heard the allegation about pulling a gun on the police who went to arrest him. Particularly when there stood beside him in the dock Burnley who, in the hearing of the jury, had pleaded guilty to receiving furs knowing them to have been stolen. For the human mind is particularly susceptible to what the logicians term the 'Fallacy of the Ten Leaking Buckets'. One leaking bucket will not hold water and everybody recognises the fact; nor will ten, but the mind frequently fails to accept that fact. A scintilla of suspicion alone about one crime, quite inadequate by itself to convict, can become, to the mind of a jury, overwhelming proof if added to similar scintillae of suspicion about other crimes. Nought plus nought plus nought becomes equated to two and two, making four. It is a danger that our courts ought particularly to guard against, but modern practice has increasingly come to permit the joinder, in one indictment and one trial, of numerous charges; and judges will all too rarely consent to a severance of the indictment or separate trials of separate allegations.

On the second charge Niven Scott Craig admitted that he had the automatic under his pillow, but he denied that he made any attempt to draw it on the officers. As to that, there was only his word against the police, for the counsel defending Niven did not call Peggy to corroborate his story, although she was the only other eye-witness of what took place in that room in Kensington Gardens Square. No doubt defending counsel thought, as I would have done, that the jury would not attach any weight to her evidence and that to call her might discredit the accused. For not only was she a partial witness, his girl-friend, but she had had convictions in the past for prostitution. The prosecution therefore would have been entitled to attack her character.

It is an unfortunate dilemma in which defending counsel are

often placed. A prosecution witness cannot be cross-examined as to previous convictions or bad character without the accused's own character being put in issue and any previous convictions he may have coming before the jury if he gives evidence; but the prosecution, even when they are not entitled to attack the character of the accused, can always go for any witnesses called for the defence. The unfairness of the rule is aggravated by the fact that judges are entitled to, and often do, invite the jury to speculate why a particular witness has not been called for the defence, with the inevitable inference that the reason is that the witness would not have supported the accused's account of events if called. Justice obviously demands that all eye-witnesses to material facts in issue should be called by the prosecution.

In this case Peggy was the wife of a Pole who had deserted her, leaving her with two young children to support. She had for a time gone on the streets. Since she had met Niven Scott Craig – many months before the night in question – she had been his mistress and he had supported her and her children. Although there was a great deal to her discredit, she was not an entirely worthless creature; and even a convicted prostitute can sometimes tell the truth. Yet what modern jury would believe even Mary Magdalene, if her previous record was before them?

Whatever the jury decided on the case of Niven Scott Craig, the Craig family believed that he had received a sentence of 12 years imprisonment for crimes he had not committed. For among other things they had seen Christopher set off with his brother on the night in question in a small hired car for a weekend's rabbit shooting in Norfolk. And they believed Peggy's version of events rather than that of the police.

If in fact Christopher had been with Niven rabbit shooting in Norfolk, he knew for certain that his brother was innocent of one of the crimes for which he was convicted.

*

Christopher Craig had jumped from the roof of Barlow & Parker's warehouse after the shooting on the night of 2 November. His fall was broken by a greenhouse, but he nevertheless

58

sustained severe injuries, fracturing his breastbone, spine and left wrist. Looking at him sitting quietly, bandaged up, in his chair in the interviewing room, it was difficult to picture him doing any of the things he had done. For the outstanding impression was one of femininity. He had dark brown eyes, soft bow-shaped lips and a smooth skin that would have passed as attractive on any girl, and his voice and manner were diffident and gentle. Perhaps his appearance was a clue to his character; that he felt a need constantly to assert to himself his own masculinity by possessing guns and emulating those he instinctively felt to be more mannish characters and, ultimately, by deeds of cruelty and violence.

His father, Niven Craig senior, was his first hero. Christopher admired him irrationally, because he had been a good rugger player and had a good war record. When he talked of how his father had been in close combat with Germans in the First World War his eyes lit up. He was proud that in 1917 his father had been rated the fourth best shot in the Army. It was his father who had first taught Christopher to shoot and who had encouraged in him a love of firearms. Christopher's enthusiasm for guns was noticed at school, and not only by the boys in front of whom he showed off. When he was fourteen he was found in possession of a starter pistol made into a lethal weapon by boring the barrel.

But the real hero of Christopher's life was his brother Niven; he worshipped him and tried to imitate him. In September 1951 Christopher disappeared from home in company with another boy. The authorities at the ports were warned that he might try to get to France and that he might be armed. The two boys were found under a boat on Brighton beach. In his pocket Christopher Craig had a Webley pistol. It was all an attempt to repeat his brother's exploit of trying to cross the Channel in an open boat – only now there was no war on and no Germans to fight. It all made a rather stupid and meaningless story when he appeared before the magistrates, charged with unlawful possession of a firearm. He was fined thirty-five shillings and the gun was confiscated.

The solicitor's secretary and I got from Craig, not without difficulty, his version of the events of the night of 2 November, or so much as he cared to tell us.

On the occasions when I saw him in prison, he was wearing a suede jacket, bright blue-grey trousers and flashy suede shoes with thick crepe soles. I told him to see that he turned up in court looking less like an American gangster.

'I haven't any other kinds of clothes,' Craig told me.

'Well, see that your father buys some for you before Tuesday – something quiet and conservative.'

*

The account Craig gave us was, I thought at the time, candid and probable.

Five youths had set out that night to rob a butcher's shop in Croydon. Derek Bentley, his co-accused, had worked as a part-time errand boy for the butcher. (In those days tradesmen still delivered their goods to customers by bicycle.) He had taken the opportunity to steal a bunch of keys from the butcher, which included not only the keys to the shop but also the keys to his safe. The other three were Norman Parsley, who was a Dulwich College boy, Frank Fazey and another youth.

When they got to the shop there was a light visible in the glass over the doorway. The butcher was in the shop, probably writing up his accounts. Some of them then turned back.

Craig and Bentley went on to break into some other premises and eventually got over the gate and up the vent pipes on to the roof of the warehouse of Barlow & Parker's premises in Tamworth Road.

It was not long afterwards that the police arrived. Detective-Constable Fairfax, in plain clothes, climbed up one of the vent pipes, told them he was a police officer and that the place was surrounded. He then arrested Bentley.

Craig claimed that at no time had he shot directly at any police officer but that he either aimed at the ground or fired over the garden of No. 30 Tamworth Road. This seemed to be borne out by the evidence of DC Fairfax in the depositions. He described how he had arrested Bentley and continued:

I then took Bentley round the stack with a view to closing in on Craig and as we got round the other side we came face to face with Craig. Craig was then on the westerly side of the stack.

Bentley then broke away from me and as he did so he shouted 'Let him have it, Chris'.

There was a loud report and a flash and something hit my shoulder which caused me to spin round and fall to the ground.

It was my shoulder which was hit.

As I was getting up I saw one man moving away on my left and one on my right.

I rushed at the man on my right, who was Bentley, and I closed on him and struck him with my fist, causing him to fall to the ground. As he did so there was a second report and a flash and I dropped down and pulled Bentley in front of me as a shield.

According to Fairfax he was 'within six feet ... face to face' with Craig. At that distance a bullet from an Eley .455, if it had struck him, would inevitably have shattered his whole shoulder or at least drilled it. In fact the medical evidence showed that the bullet had hit his shoulder, travelled over it without piercing any part of the skin and gone down his back and lodged in his trouser top. It was clearly a spent bullet, from a ricochet from the ground.

*

Craig thought that he had killed PC Miles, as he does apparently to this day. But at the time he wondered how this could have happened. He had a .455 Eley revolver, from which he had cut part of the barrel so that he could put it in his pocket. The bullets he had were for the most part tommy-gun bullets of .45 calibre, so that they were not a perfect fit. For these two reasons, his weapon was wildly inaccurate.

Of the prosecution evidence contained in the depositions, he totally denied that Bentley had ever broken away from DC Fairfax after he had been arrested or that he had said the words 'Let him have it, Chris'.

He also denied that he had made some of the damning observations reported by police officers: 'I am Craig. You've just given my brother twelve years. Come on, you coppers, I'm only sixteen. Come on, you brave coppers, think of your wives.'

He was also, according to the depositions, alleged to have said to police officers waiting by his bedside to record his observations: 'I had six in the gun. I fired at a policeman. I had six tommy-gun bullets.' And later, 'Is the copper dead? How about the others? I ought to have shot the lot.'

An inspector arrived and charged him with the murder of PC Miles. His only comment was: 'He's dead, is he? What about the others?'

He fell into a drugged sleep, but in the early hours of the morning he opened his eyes. A uniformed policeman sat by his bedside.

'Did I really kill a policeman?' he asked. 'I got the gun from a house at Purley. There are plenty more where that came from.'

He was operated on later that morning, under anaesthetic. In the course of the afternoon, when he was in great pain, he was alleged to have said: 'You coppers. The other one's dead with a hole in his head. I'm all right. All you bastards should be dead.'

Half an hour later, he suddenly asked: 'Is he dead?'

'Who?'

'That copper. I shot him in the head and he went down like a ton of bricks.'

Three days later he made a further observation, which a police officer noted down:

'If I hadn't cut a bit off the barrel of my gun I would probably have killed a lot more policemen. That night I was out to kill because I had so much hate inside me for what they did to my brother.'

*

Craig imparted one item of information to me which was of great importance – not to him but to Bentley. That was that Fairfax, having arrested Bentley and while both of them were sheltering behind the roof lights, sent Bentley out to get the gun from

5. Christopher Craig

Craig. This was early on, certainly before Miles was shot.

Bentley went out and got within six feet of Craig, when Craig said to him, 'Fuck off, otherwise I'll shoot you, too.' This means that it must have taken place after Fairfax had suffered his trifling injury from a shot from Craig.

Craig only told me this on the second day I saw him, the Sunday, but I immediately realised the significance of it. It showed that far from inciting Craig to shoot at police officers, Bentley was actively engaged in trying to stop it.

I told Craig in no uncertain terms that that piece of evidence was of crucial importance for the defence of Bentley, but that I didn't propose to lead him in evidence about it for two reasons. First, it showed him in a very bad light, as one willing to injure or kill his own mate. Secondly, it was totally destructive of his own defence that he was only firing on the ground or over the garden of No. 30 Tamworth Road, in order to frighten off the police, and that the death of PC Miles was accidental. But I put it to him very strongly that he should consent to my telling Bentley's counsel, Frank Cassels, all about it, and that if Frank cross-examined him about it he should tell the truth. To this he agreed.

It is interesting to note that when David Yallop interviewed Christopher Craig in the course of research for his book *To Encourage the Others* (1971), Craig confirmed this. Yallop claims that Craig told him:

To me one of the most terrible things that happened was Bentley turning against me. Helping the police like that. They got him to come over to me to persuade me to give myself up. Bentley walked over to me and called out 'For Christ's sake, Chris, what's got into you?' I realised what he was up to and told him to stop or he'd get it too. Bentley stopped for a moment, then started to move towards me, not in a straight line, but as if he was trying to work his way behind me. I told him that I knew what he was up to, that he was trying to get behind me to get at the gun. Again he asked me, 'What's got into you, Chris?' I told him, 'Get back or I'll shoot you. For a moment I thought he was still going to come on. Then he turned and walked back to the police.

Yallop interviewed Fairfax and questioned him about this incident. Fairfax was not prepared to deny that it had happened, but he claimed he could not recall it.

Armed with this information, I went to have a joint conference with Bentley's counsel Frank Cassels. I was rather surprised when his opening words were 'I think both little fuckers ought to swing', spoken with considerable venom. Later, when I wrote briefly about the case in my book *Most of My Murders*, I softened his words to 'I think both little beggers ought to swing'. Subsequently he admitted to a journalist in an interview with the *Croydon Post* in June 1987, and in an earlier interview with David Yallop in 1970, that he had told me 'I think both little bastards ought to swing.'

His attitude was fairly representative of the vast majority of the British public at that time. When Craig was brought on a stretcher to appear at the committal proceedings in the magistrates' court, the police had great difficulty in preventing him being lynched by the crowd.

Because Frank said that to me at the time is no reason for M.J. Trow to write in his account of the case, *Let him have it, Chris* (1990): 'If he really meant it, then surely there is at least room for the question: how hard did he try?' Still less for David Yallop to comment: 'It indicated a remarkable lack of commitment.' When Yallop interviewed him in 1970 or thereabouts, Frank had not changed his views. He still thought that 'anybody who carries a gun and kills a policeman ought to hang'.

The implied suggestion of both these authors that Frank did not do his best for his client is a grotesque slur on the memory of an honourable man and shows a total ignorance of the ethics and obligations of the Bar. A lot of accused persons would go undefended if counsel could only defend those they believed to be innocent. As Fenton Bresler commented:

'It would be a bad day for the independence of the Bar and the quality of our justice if counsel were only to represent causes with which privately they were in sympathy and persons for whom, as individuals, they had feelings of liking or affection.'

6

Frank Cassels and Derek Bentley

Francis Cassels was the son of Mr Justice ('Jimmy') Cassels, one of the most amiable and pleasant judges on the High Court Bench. Jimmy Cassels had, I believe, started life as an errand boy in Liverpool, learnt typing and shorthand at night school and become a journalist, and then read for the Bar in his spare time. Perhaps because of his background, he was entirely free from the arrogance and bad temper which characterises so many on the High Court Bench. In those days there were some real bastards on the Bench, of whom most counsel were justly afraid. Apart from Goddard, who was the supreme Bully on the Bench, one of these was Mr Justice Croom-Johnson, who presided over Bentley's appeal. As Harry Hylton-Foster once remarked, he was a small man whose delight and mission in life were to try to make big men look small.

Another of whom the Bar went in fear was Mr Justice Hallett, who in one case asked more questions than both counsel put together and was rightly accused by the Court of Appeal of descending into the arena of the conflict. He was so clever and conscious of his cleverness that his particular pleasure was to expose any counsel before him as bloody fools. As Rudolph Lyons warned me early in my pupillage, 'there is no other profession where grown men are so publicly insulted and humiliated'.

Another who terrorised the Bar was Mr Justice Oliver, who was cold and deadly to the defence on all occasions and whose summings-up were rich in venom against any accused. His speciality was writing down what a witness had *not* said in a form most deadly to the accused and then asking the witness if his note was correct. They always, of course, said that it was.

These and others intimidated most of the Bar, but they did not intimidate me and I had stand-up rows in court with all of them, so that in time they came to leave me well alone. But as Rudolph repeatedly warned me, 'You expose yourself too much for your clients.'

As it happened, in time I came to be quite good friends with Hallett who had me into his room once in a rape case to tell me and counsel for the prosecution that my cross-examination was the most masterly he had ever heard in such a case. He persuaded the prosecution to drop the case. I became even better friends with Oliver; so much so that I was known on the Circuit as 'Oliver's Blue-eyed Boy'. In part, that may have been due to the fact that in a Union Debate at Durham University I had moved a resolution to the effect that 'the attitude of the Church to divorce is unchristian'. Oliver was the only judge in the High Court who had been a co-respondent in a divorce case. He had earned a VC in the First World War and lost an eye, and that was held to outweigh his moral deliquency, as it was then regarded. So friendly was I with him that he invited me to undo his fly buttons in the urinal of the Leeds Club when he was too pissed to do it himself.

Mr Justice Cassels had none of the characteristics of any of these, and his son had inherited his genial character. Frank was a thoroughly decent and honest man but, I fear, did not inherit his father's great talents as an advocate. His father had appeared in some of the most famous murder trials while he was at the Bar. This was, so far as I know, the first and only time Frank was instructed for the defence in a murder trial.

*

As we have seen, a number of non-legal writers have since criticised Frank for the way he handled the defence of Bentley. Most of this criticism is totally unfair and unjustified. The authors concerned have not had the least idea of the parameters within which a defence counsel has to operate.

To start with, he is bound by the instructions he receives from his client. In this case both Bentley and Craig admitted to their counsel that it was a shot from the revolver fired by Craig that had killed PC Miles. Therefore there was no reason for either of us to cross-examine the pathologist about the dimensions of the bullet that had killed the officer, even if he had been in any position to determine that. Craig to this day accepts that it was a shot from his gun that was the cause of the officer's death.

Secondly, defence counsel is precluded from interviewing any witnesses of fact apart from his own client. He is not there to carry out a probing investigation such as feature in who-dunnit American television programmes.

Finally, neither he nor his solicitor has any facilities to search out and interview witnesses in the way the police have. That was certainly the position under the Poor Prisoners' Defence Act when both counsel and solicitors received contemptible remuneration, which resulted in their not only not receiving a fair recompense for their time, but incurring substantial expenses for which they were not compensated in any way. Frank received £10 for his defence of Bentley and £11 for the appeal to the Court of Criminal Appeal.

In this case John Stevens, his instructing solicitor, had done a lot of work on the case and produced a thorough brief and proof of the evidence of his client, together with medical reports. These latter all came from the prison doctor, for the simple reason that the defence of Bentley had not the time, the opportunity or the resources to instruct an independent consultant to examine him.

Frank has been criticised for not making greater use of them, but in truth they were completely irrelevant to the only issue before the court, his client's innocence or guilt of the crime of murder. There are two ways in which at that time they could have been relevant: if Bentley was insane under the McNaghton rules; or if he was unfit to plead so that he was unable to instruct counsel or comprehend the nature of the proceedings. There was no question of either. A third way in which it might have been relevant was if he could have been certified under the Mental Deficiency Acts. As to that, Frank had no evidence that Bentley's mental intelligence was below that prescribed by statute. In the circumstances, the most that any defending counsel could hope for in the case was what in fact Frank achieved: a recommendation to mercy from the jury.

*

There is no doubt, however, that Frank had big problems with his client, because he was a moron.

Bentley was born on 3 June 1933, one of unexpected twins. The other, delivered later, died within two hours. At the age of four he apparently fell off a lorry, which triggered an epileptic fit at the time and minor fits later. From August 1941 to December 1943 he went to Camrose Avenue School, Islington. Twice subsequently the family home was destroyed in air raids, and on the second occasion he was buried in debris before being pulled out by rescue workers. At eleven, when he went to the John Ruskin School at Walworth, it was discovered that he was totally illiterate. In 1945 the family moved to Norbury and he went to the school where he met Christopher Craig, Norbury Manor.

It was a school notorious for its ferocious discipline. The Headmaster of that time was reported in the local paper, under the headline SCHOOL WHERE THE CANE IS USED – NO DISCI-PLINARY PROBLEM as saying:

> We use the cane ... We are still old-fashioned enough to believe that if a boy rides over the traces then he should be made to realise that punishment is going to be swift and automatic. I don't recall one boy who has resented corporal punishment.

But Bentley was a frequent truant, and he was brought before local magistrates for this. He was then, on their orders, transferred to another secondary school, Ingrams. Four months later, he was transferred back to Norbury Manor, still illiterate, as he remained to the end of his life. 'If he attended once a week, we were lucky,' the deputy head at the time told a reporter later. After ten months, he was transferred back to Ingrams under an attendance order made by local magistrates. Five months later, in January 1948, he was back at Norbury Manor. The deputy head described him as 'like a great lump of lard, an utterly worthless piece of humanity'.

In March 1948 he appeared with another boy at Croydon Juvenile Court and was found guilty of two offences: attempting to break-and-enter and attempting to steal ten shillings and a quantity of bus tickets from a conductor's box. He was bound over for two years and another attendance order was made on him, to go to Ingrams School. It was the ninth move in his scholastic career. He left school the following summer. It was not long before he appeared again before the local magistrates, this time for stealing tools from a building site. He was sentenced to a third year term at an Approved School.

He went to the Kingswood School at Bristol where he was given an IQ test which resulted in a reading of 66 on the Stanford-Binet scale, then classed as 'feeble-minded'. The school reported that 'he reserved his energy only for eating and talking; that he was self-satisfied, indifferent to training and content to let others do the work'. From there he was released before the expiration of the full period of his sentence on 28 July 1950.

The following year he began to work with a firm of furniture removers but gave it up in March 1952, shortly after he was due to be called up for compulsory National Service. At his medical examination he was placed in the lowest grade, IV, as being mentally sub-normal. He had a brief period of subsequent employment as a dustman and a road-sweeper but was dismissed because he was unreliable and a bad time-keeper.

*

Not only was Bentley a moron but he was a lying moron. He denied in the witness box that Craig and he had gone out that evening with the intention of breaking in anywhere. His evidence at the trial when he was asked by the judge about his movements on the fatal night was as follows:

Where were you going?

Just to Croydon, sir

Yes, but what for?

Just for the ride, sir, an ordinary ride.

Just for a ride?

I used to go down to Croydon a lot.

I dare say you did, but you said that on this night you met Craig, stood on the corner talking, and then jumped on a bus. What did you jump on a bus for?

Well, if we go the other way there is nothing there; it is all quiet, so we went Croydon way, sir.

What were you going to do at Croydon?

Just walk around.

It was obviously and patently untrue. He might have been more convincing in his denial of the use of the crucial words 'Let him have it, Chris' if he had told the truth and frankly confessed that they had gone out that night to break into the butcher's shop but had been deterred because of the light above the door. The truth might have persuaded the jury that neither youth had any intention of breaking into any occupied premises, still less to use violence.

He lied about knowing the purpose for which he and Craig had gone over the six-foot-high gate. He replied to his counsel as follows:

Had you and Craig up to that time made any arrangement to break in anywhere?

No, sir.

Where did you get off the bus?

West Croydon Station.

Did anything happen on the bus between you and Craig?

Yes, he gave me a pair of knuckledusters.

Is that the knuckleduster which has been produced in court?

Yes.

Had you seen that before?

No.

What did you do with it when he gave it to you?

70

Just put it in my pocket.

When you got off the bus at Croydon, where did you go?

We crossed over, and went down Tamworth Road.

That is the road in which the warehouse is situated?

That is right.

At that time had you made any arrangement to break into anywhere?

No, sir.

What happened after that?

We went down to Reeves' Corner, sir; we walked down to Reeves' Corner and crossed over, and then we came back up.

Would that bring you back past this particular warehouse?

Yes.

At that point Goddard intervened:

You walked down Tamworth Road and then came back?

Yes, sir; we went to Reeves' and then crossed over and came back.

What is Reeves?

Salesrooms, sir.

What time of night was this – half past nine?

Yes.

Cassels continued:

Is Reeves' salesroom on the other side of the road to this warehouse?

Yes.

Then you crossed the road and came back again past the warehouse?

Yes, that is right.

What happened when you got there?

We looked into the window of the sweetstuff shop.

What happened next?

I was still looking in it, and Craig had got over this iron fence.

Once again Goddard intervened:

> Without ever saying anything to you?
> No, sir, I was still looking into the window.
> I see. Craig got over the fence without saying anything to you, did he?
> Yes, sir.

Cassels at this point was allowed to continue his examination:

> What did you do?
> I walked to the end of the kerb.
> And what next?
> I followed then, sir.
> You followed him over the fence?
> Yes.
> Why was that?
> I could not answer that.

Goddard was swiftly in with an exclamation full of incredulity and disbelief, with a significant nod to the jury:

> What!?
> I do not know, I just went.
> Well, you were going to break in, were you not?
> I do not know why I went over the fence, though.
> You do not know why you went over the fence?
> No, sir.

That, again, was such evident lies that no sensible jury would give any credence to anything else he said.

*

Bentley lied about knowing whether Craig had a gun, and he persisted in that obvious lie. Craig had carried a gun with him ever since he was eleven. At school, it compensated for the mickey that was taken out of him because he was the dunce of any form he was in and could not read or write. Even his teachers knew this and did not think it a serious matter, certainly not as serious as carrying a knife which could do serious damage, as one of them put it.

Of course Bentley knew that Craig had a gun. He knew that he was never without one. But, I believe, he never thought for one moment that Craig would ever use it.

*

Counsel, presented with a proof of evidence prepared by a solicitor which contains *obvious* lies which no jury is likely to accept, is in a dilemma.

To start with, most statements of accused in those days were taken down by a 15-year-old typist or an articled clerk or anybody the solicitor's office could spare. If the office cat could write, it would have been sent. (The situation is not much different in these days under legal aid.) As a result, the statements rarely addressed the real issues of the case or provided adequate information against the allegations of the prosecution.

However, unlike my instructing solicitor who had never seen his client, John Stevens had spent a lot of time on his client's case, had briefed Frank fully and had given him a complete proof of evidence and all medical reports. I have no idea whether Frank ever saw his own client, but there was no obligation on him to do so. I do know that he did not go, as I did, on to the roof of the warehouse in question. Not that my visit assisted me at the time, although some of the things I noticed then may have a significance in the light of subsequent discoveries about the case (see pp. 160–1 below).

Counsel is bound by the instructions given by his client. He is not there to invent a defence for him, still less to run a case which is not consistent with his instructions. But what is he to do when his client proposes to tell obvious lies which no jury is likely to accept?

There were various techniques I learned from my seniors and betters who from time to time led me when I was a junior. One approach was that of a learned counsel who has recently retired as a judge. He tapped the proof of evidence carefully typed up by the solicitor and said to the accused: 'Look, this is a load of balls. Don't tell me a pack of fucking lies. *I'm paid to tell the lies.* Now tell me what really happened.'

A more subtle method was used by Harry Hylton-Foster QC. As befitted an Old Etonian, his approach was more suave. 'This really won't do,' he said plaintively, pointing to the proof of the accused. 'No jury's going to believe this. Why don't you tell me the truth? Now isn't this what happened ... .' He then propounded a quite new and plausible defence. In one case in which he was leading me, there were two co-defendants.

'And at that point the defences are bifurcated,' Harry told our client.

'What, already!' exclaimed the client in dismay. He apparently thought the word was a synonym for a more familiar one.

*

I had this problem the first time I appeared for the defence of Anthony O'Rourke. He was charged with the murder of an old man by striking him across the head with a poker. The proof of his evidence prepared by the solicitor contained a denial that he had been anywhere near the house in which the killing took place at the time. There was substantial evidence against this: a letter he had written to his unmarried 'wife', a statement made to the police, and two witnesses, one of whom had seen him going to the house and the other coming from it, and the fact that he had run away afterwards. Also the fact that he had cashed a tobacco coupon belonging to the old man.

When I saw O'Rourke in the glass cage at Armley Prison, with a warder on a chair outside, I told him frankly what I thought.

'You're in a bit of a spot,' I said to him.

'Sure,' he agreed in his quiet Irish brogue.

'And this bloody nonsense just won't do,' I said, pointing at the statement carefully typed up by his solicitor.

'No?' he said, politely and without the least surprise.

From the depositions I went through all the evidence against him and cross-examined him on his story, as I knew he would be cross-examined by the prosecution should he persist in that version. He agreed in the end it wouldn't do and we tore up the proof of his evidence. By the time I left him he had promised to write out in his own hand a full account of what really did transpire.

The following Sunday when I saw him again he had prepared several sheets of prison paper with his new version on it. In this account he admitted that he had been in the dead man's house, and that a quarrel had arisen about the virtue of the woman O'Rourke referred to as his wife, or rather her lack of it; and he said that the dead man had seized the poker in order to strike him but he had grabbed it from him and struck him first.

The jury were left by Mr Justice Streatfeild with three possible verdicts. First, murder; secondly, manslaughter, if the jury thought he had been grossly and suddenly provoked by an assault, such as would cause a reasonable man to lose control and strike out while his 'blood was up'; or thirdly, not guilty, if they thought O'Rourke had struck the blow in self-defence while he was unable to escape and when his own life was in peril. He was acquitted of both murder and manslaughter and walked out of the dock a free man.

Eighteen months later, he was back in the dock charged with the murder of an old woman. On that occasion, at 6.30 one morning he walked into a police station, said he had killed her and asked for me. At the subsequent trial he was acquitted of murder but convicted of manslaughter.

*

A week after the trial of Craig and Bentley had ended, Leonard Parkin, later to become a TV news reader, who was then court reporter in Leeds for the *Yorkshire Evening News*, and who had covered the trial at the Old Bailey, was kind enough to say to me, 'If you had defended Bentley instead of Craig, I think he would not have been convicted.'

I told him I thought it doubtful whether anybody could have successfully defended Bentley. Even if the police had been so discredited that the jury did not accept that he had said 'Let him have it, Chris', there remained the undisputed evidence from which a joint venture could have been inferred. If two people go out to commit a crime, one armed with a revolver and ammunition and a knife, and the other with a knuckleduster and a knife, any jury would be entitled to infer that they had agreed to use violent means to resist arrest if necessary.

Further, the capitulation and arrest of Bentley did not necessarily end the joint venture. The *consequences* of it and responsibility for it could continue even though one party to it had surrendered to the police, if the other had been continuing the violence to which both had previously agreed.

The burden rested on the prosecution to prove to the jury beyond reasonable doubt that the two youths had, expressly or impliedly, agreed to use what violence was necessary to escape arrest. The mere possession of weapons by both raised a *prima facie* presumption of prior agreement.

But that evidence of prior agreement could have been rebutted by evidence which the jury accepted from the accused that there was no agreement to use violence. For that Bentley would have had to be a lot more candid with the jury and a lot more truthful than he was apparently prepared to be. He would have had to admit frankly in evidence that they had gone out intending to break into the butcher's shop. He would have had to admit that, of course, when they tried to break into the warehouse they were intent on stealing whatever they could lay their hands on.

He also would have had to admit that he knew that Craig always carried a gun, even on the most innocuous trips. But he could, truthfully, have said that he never thought for one moment that Craig would be stupid enough to use it. It was just youthful bravado, an attempt to compensate for his manifest inadequacies.

It is probable that, frightened and moronic as he was, he would not have agreed.

*

Had I been defending Bentley I would have used the first police officer who gave evidence to try to establish two things: first, that the late PC Miles was a highly regarded and well-liked member of the police force in 'J' division of the Metropolitan Police stationed at the Croydon station; secondly, that the whole station were outraged and deeply distressed by the murder of their colleague. I would have tried to get him to agree that the attitude of *every* member of the station was that of the general public, who at that stage thought, as did Frank Cassels, that both little bastards ought to swing.

The first officer from the Croydon station to give evidence was a PC Charles Beard. He was a young man who produced a plan he had prepared of the layout of the roof of Barlow & Parker's warehouse. No doubt he would not have expected any cross-examination and, being naive and inexperienced, would have truthfully answered questions relating to the state of mind of police officers in Croydon station after the death of PC Miles: anger and rage and frustration because they knew the principal criminal would not hang. Although counsel for the defence would not have any information regarding PC Miles, this officer would undoubtedly have volunteered everything about him.

Miles had been commended three times for gallantry in effecting arrests, the most recent case being in 1941. He had played football and cricket for the Croydon Police Athletic Club. He was, as one of his colleagues said at the time, 'a good type and a good efficient officer'. He was an immaculate football full-back who had never fouled a man on the pitch in his life. Another colleague said of him at the time: 'Sidney had been a long time in the force ... everybody liked him.' No doubt PC Beard would have accepted all this and the outrage the whole station felt about his murder – thereby providing evidence of a reason why officers from that station should have lied against Bentley.

I should also have asked him the apparently innocuous question: 'I take it that, as in all police stations, there is a copy of *Moriarty's Police Law* in the Fells Road Station?' Of course there was. It was the Bible of every copper.

*

77

The prosecution did not really rely on the evidence of a joint venture which could be inferred from the possession of instruments of violence. That was only a 'fall-back' position. What they really relied on was the proposition that Derek Bentley, *after* his arrest, had invited Christopher Craig to shoot at DC Fairfax by using the words 'Let him have it, Chris'. By implication that was an incitement for Craig to use the weapon Bentley undoubtedly knew Craig possessed to shoot DC Fairfax: therefore, by implication to shoot at *any* police officer including the unfortunate PC Miles.

However, as the present Lord Chief Justice, Lord Lane, said in the case of the 'Guildford Four', when the Criminal Division of the Court of Appeal in October 1989 quashed the conviction of four Irish persons alleged to have planted a bomb in a Guildford pub: 'Any evidence which casts real doubt on the reliability or veracity of the officers responsible for the various interrogations has to mean that the whole foundation of the prosecution case disappears, and the convictions will be unsafe.'

In Bentley's case, I believed at the time and still believe that it could have been possible to instill in the minds of the jury real doubts about the reliability and veracity of the officers responsible for the evidence against Bentley.

An old and experienced counsel, the late Paley Scott KC, used to say: 'If you're going to attack the credibility of the police, you've either got to piss or get off the pot.' Frank Cassels chose early to get off the pot. It was not an adequate defence of his client simply in cross-examination to say to Fairfax, Harrison and McDonald, the three police officers who swore that those words had been used (although McDonald was not prepared to swear that they had been used by Bentley), 'I put it to you those words were not said.'

I'm afraid that had I defended Bentley I should certainly have pissed in the pot and on their evidence. But it would have enraged Lord Goddard, who was determined to get both convicted of murder, and it would have led to even more interruptions by him – according to Fenton Bresler he intervened 250 times in the course of the trial – and to several stand-up rows with him.

6. Frank Cassels and Derek Bentley

*

The police officers were certainly vulnerable to an attack on their credibility, because two of them were undoubtedly lying. Even the prosecution did not accept that they were telling the truth.

After he had been taken and put in a cell in Fells Road Police Station, Bentley some time later was brought up before Detective Chief Inspector Smith and Detective-Sergeant Shepherd. He had, according to them, voluntarily and spontaneously made a statement which was written down by Shepherd. It read:

STATEMENT OF: DEREK WILLIAM BENTLEY, age 19

> 1 Fairview Road, London Road
> Norbury

Electrician

who saith:
I have been cautioned that I need not say anything unless I wish to do so, but whatever I do say will be taken down in writing and may be given in evidence.

> (signed) Derek Bentley

I have known Craig since I went to school. We were stopped by our parents going out together, but we still continued going out with each other – I mean we have not gone out together until tonight.

I was watching television tonight [2 November 1952] and between 8 p.m. and 9 p.m. Craig called for me. My mother answered the door and I heard her say that I was out. I had been out earlier to the pictures and got home just after 7 p.m.

A little later Norman Parsley and Frank Fazey called. I did not answer the door. Mother told me that they had called and I then ran out after them. I walked up the road with them to the paper shop where I saw Craig standing. We all talked together and then Norman Parsley and Frank

Fazey left. Chris Craig and I then caught a bus to Croydon. We got off at West Croydon and then we walked down the road where the toilets are – I think it is Tamworth Road. When we came to the place where you found me, Chris looked in the window. There was a little iron gate at the side. Chris then jumped over and I followed. Chris then climbed up the drainpipe to the roof and I followed. Up to then Chris had not said anything. We both got out on to the flat roof at the top. Then someone in a garden on the opposite side shone a torch towards us. Chris said, 'It's a copper, hide behind here.' We hid behind a shelter arrangement on the roof. We were there waiting for about ten minutes. I did not know he was going to use the gun.

A plain clothes man climbed up the drainpipe and on to the roof. The man said, 'I am a police officer – the place is surrounded.' He caught hold of me and as we walked away Chris fired. There was nobody else there at the time. The policeman and I then went round a corner by a door.

A little later the door opened and a policeman in uniform came out. Chris fired again then and this policeman fell down. I could see that he was hurt as a lot of blood came from his forehead just above his nose. The policemen dragged him round the corner behind the brickwork entrance to the door. I remember I shouted something but I forget what it was. I could not see Chris when I shouted to him – he was behind a wall. I heard some more policemen behind the door and the policeman with me said, 'I don't think he has many more bullets left.' Chris shouted, 'Oh yes I have,' and he fired again. I think I heard him fire three times altogether. The policeman then pushed me down the stairs and I did not see any more.

I knew we were going to break into the place. I did not know what we were going to get – just anything that was going. I did not have a gun and I did not know Chris had one until he shot. I now know that the policeman in uniform that was shot is dead.

I should have mentioned that after the plain clothes policeman got up the drainpipe and arrested me, another policeman in uniform followed and I heard someone call him 'Mac'. He was with us when the other policeman was killed.

This statement has been read to me and it is true
(signed) Derek W Bentley

Statement taken by me [Smith], written down by Detective Sergeant Shepherd, read over and signature witnessed by J. Smith, Detective Chief Inspector.

That at least is the version published in the Notable British Trials series. It omits two crucial facts.

The original statement included the words

tis as B
This statement has been read to me and is true
Derk Derek W. Bentley

'Derk' was Bentley's attempt to spell his own name; 'tis as B' his attempt to write 'This statement has been read to me ...'.

Moreover, in the original document Bentley is purported to have signed his name six times, with three of these signatures witnessed by 'J.S.' – Detective Chief Inspector John Smith. Bentley's signature appears in three versions: Derek Bentley, D. Bentley and Derek W. Bentley. A true signature is invariably the same.

The inescapable conclusion is that the two police officers forged Bentley's signature no less than six times.

Both officers swore on oath that Bentley had dictated the statement to them *without any questions from them*. That was because, by the Judges' Rules of that time, once an accused had been arrested or police officers had made up their mind to charge him, they should not question him. There were also two cases to the same effect.

It was strictly required that the time when the accused began to make his statement and the time when he finished should be recorded. There were no times on the document.

There was material there for making a rigorous attack in cross-examination on the credibility of the two police officers. Their evidence was that this was a spontaneous direct voluntary statement made by Bentley and not in answer to questions from the officers. Why then did he refer to his friend as 'Craig' in the very first sentence? If they had been Bentley's words it would have been 'Chris'. All the words are those of police jargon. Particularly is this true of observations like 'I now know ...'. Literate people, let alone 19-year-old illiterates, do not use language like that.

Even more significant is the number of negatives in the statement. A person who is making a spontaneous voluntary statement does not refer to what did not happen. He speaks only of what did. But a person answering questions will deny things.

Undoubtedly, I would have invited the jury to consider whether they could possibly accept the evidence of Detective-Sergeant Shepherd and Detective Chief Inspector Smith. If those two police officers did not scruple to forge the signatures on an accused's statement, neither they nor other officers would have scrupled to fabricate words alleged to have been said by Bentley – 'putting the verbal on', as it is termed.

Even the prosecution did not believe them when they swore that the statement had not been made without Bentley having been questioned.

At one stage in his cross-examination by Humphreys, Bentley said about part of his statement: 'That was in answer to a question.'

Humphreys replied: *'I dare say it was in reply to a question.* It was written down and read over to you?'

Later in the cross-examination Humphreys asked: 'What are you suggesting then – that a police officer writes down something you did not say?'

To this Bentley replied: 'He asked me a question there, sir', to which Humphreys responded: *'I dare say he did ask you a question,* but he has sworn he wrote down what you said.'

There was also a curious feature which was inexplicable at the time. The sentence: 'I should have mentioned that after the plain clothes policeman got up the drainpipe and arrested me another policeman in uniform followed and I heard someone call him "Mac".' There may be significance in it in the light of evidence not available at the time. One of the police officers who was undoubtedly there at the time has since protested that McDonald was never on the roof.

*

The prosecution's case was as neat and tidy and as well rehearsed as a stage play; which indeed it was. Detective Chief Inspector Smith, who was in charge of the case, had all his witnesses at several meetings in front of a blackboard where they decided where each was supposed to be and what he said and did. It was he, in my view, who was responsible for arranging the evidence that was responsible for convicting Derek Bentley.

I would have cross-examined him as to whether he had consulted the copy of *Moriarty's Police Law* which it had been established was available in the Croydon Police Station. I doubt that he would have denied it but, accomplished liar as he was, he might have done so. In which case, I would have cross-examined him closely on what books about criminal law were available in the station.

He would no doubt have denied that he had looked up the law about joint liability. I would have referred to the note there about *R* v. *Appleby*. In that case two men, Appleby and Ostler, broke into a warehouse. They were surprised by a police officer. Appleby was not armed, but Ostler had a gun and fired at the officer after Appleby had shouted 'Let him have it, he's alone'. The officer had stated this in an admissible declaration on his deathbed. As a result of those words Appleby, who had not fired the shot, was hanged.

I would then have drawn his attention to the *extraordinary* coincidence that in the only other case of joint liability this century exactly the same words had been used. 'Let him have it ...' were the words that hanged Appleby. Precisely the same words were alleged to have been used by Bentley. I would have suggested that he had looked the law up and told his officers to put them in the mouth of Bentley.

The two principal witnesses who claimed they had heard Bentley use the words 'Let him have it, Chris' were DC Fairfax and PC Harrison. I am afraid I would have challenged the accounts of both. Fairfax claimed initially that Bentley had broken away from him after his arrest *before* the first shot was fired. Later, in reply to counsel for the prosecution, he claimed it was *after* the first shot was fired. However, when cross-examined about it by Frank Cassels, he said: 'If I did, I have made a mistake, because Bentley actually broke away from me before the shot was fired.'

Fairfax also claimed to have knocked Bentley to the ground. During the trial, Bentley's father was kept outside the court with the overcoat his son was wearing that night. Frank apparently did not wish to call him in evidence because if he did so he would lose the last word. If I had been defending Bentley, I would have cross-examined Fairfax about the state of the roof of the warehouse that night. It was undoubtedly dirty, with the filth of years of London grit upon it, and it had been raining recently; yet the camel-hair coat Bentley was wearing that night was immaculate. I would have produced it to Fairfax and asked him to identify it.

The evidence of Harrison merited even closer examination.

*

The one element that was neglected in Cassels' cross-examination was the time factor. If both officers arrived at the same time in the same car, as they claimed, it is inconceivable that Harrison could possibly have done what he claimed to have done in time to hear the words that Bentley was claimed to have used.

According to Harrison, he and Fairfax arrived at the warehouse together in the same vehicle. (This incidentally is disputed by PC Claude Pain who, undoubtedly, was there at the time. He asserts that Harrison went there on his bicycle.) Fairfax had got over the gate and a distance of 39 feet to the vent pipe up which he climbed.

Harrison's evidence was that he had gone right round to the back of the premises to Upper Drayton Place, climbed a fence and then in some unspecified fashion got on to the sloping glass and asbestos part of the warehouse roof near the chimney stack, crawled across it and dropped down into the garden of No. 26 Tamworth Road, roused the occupants and gone through their house to Tamworth Road. He returned through the house and climbed from that garden on to the asbestos roof adjacent to it. How he climbed on to the roof is something of a mystery, since there was no convenient vent or drainpipe anywhere in the region. He then claimed to have gone along to the other part of the roof near the chimney stack. From there he claimed not only to have heard the fatal words used – some sixty feet away – but also to have seen everything that happened.

This extraordinary athletic ability merited comment, but more particularly as to the time that it took him to perform all this. The prosecution's case was that Fairfax was 'within six feet … face to face' at the time when Craig first fired. It was to the left of the lift shaft and within minutes of that officer getting on to the roof. Yet Harrison claimed to have heard it from more than sixty feet away on the roof behind No. 25 Tamworth Road and *to have seen it all*. His vision must have been almost as extraordinary as his agility. Not only was it pitch black: so dark that Fairfax was within two yards of the youths before he could see them. But from Harrison's position near the chimney stack, the left of the lift shaft was invisible. He placed the incident when Fairfax was hit as being not behind the lift shaft but somewhere behind the rooflights toward the staircase head. In that, his evidence conflicted with that of Fairfax and, in fairness, Cassels did try to pursue this point, but he was heavily obstructed by Goddard.

*

It was Mr Justice Travers Humphreys – father of Christmas Humphreys – who wrote in his memoirs, after years on the bench:

'One police officer may tell the truth, but four or five never do.' When there are several police officers, there is always a weak link in the chain and it is for defence counsel to put the maximum pressure on that.

In this case, it was PC McDonald. He was a patently uneasy witness. A reluctant perjurer, I concluded. He was fat and flabby, and I did not believe that he could ever successfully have climbed over the gate, let alone up a vent pipe. He refused to say that he had heard *Bentley* say the words 'Let him have it, Chris'. He claimed to have heard those words used, but he refused to attribute them to Bentley, although pressurised to do so by both the prosecution and the judge. He did say he had heard the words spoken by somebody while he was in the alleyway at the foot of a vent pipe. Notwithstanding his refusal, Lord Goddard later told the jury that *three* witnesses had sworn that they heard Bentley say it.

My view then and now is that McDonald did not at any time manage to get over the six-foot gate into the passage way, still less manage to climb up any vent pipe on to the roof. Had I been defending Bentley, I would have liked to invite him to perform these feats again before the jury. Goddard would, of course, have refused to allow such a test, but the request alone might well have had its effect on a jury.

Unfortunately Bentley had accepted that McDonald got on to the roof before PC Miles was shot. How did he know? Only because he was told so by the police.

Frank Cassels compounded the error. He asked his client: 'Now do you remember when the first police officer, apart from Sergeant Fairfax came over the rail?'

'Yes,' replied Bentley. 'I have forgotten his name now.'

'Never mind about his name; it was McDonald,' said Frank.

*

One thing is quite certain. Had I defended Bentley, I would have made use of the information Craig had given me to the effect that Fairfax had sent Bentley to get the gun off Craig and Craig had threatened to shoot him. For it showed conclusively that, far

86

from inciting Craig to fire, Bentley was trying hard to get the gun off him *before Miles was killed*.

But there may well have been a good reason why Cassels did not.

*

The day of the trial dawned. I arrived at the Old Bailey by bus, laden up with my red bag containing my wig box, collar box and tabs, and a briefcase with the documents.

At that moment a Rolls-Royce glided up to the side door of the Old Bailey and disgorged Captain (as he liked to call himself) Niven Craig and his wife, the parents of my client Christopher Craig, and their daughter Lucy Craig, Harry Proctor of the *Sunday Pictorial* and his assistant, Madeleine McLoughlin.

7

The Trial

Harry Proctor stood on the pavement at the entrance to the Old Bailey with the Craig family. He had a genial, proprietorial air, as if he owned not only the Craig family but the Old Bailey and the whole circus inside.

'Just one apiece, boys,' he grinned to the mob of waiting photographers. 'And no questions.' As always, Harry's suit was creased and bulging. As it well might, since he habitually carried half-bottles of brandy in his side pockets.

Later he was to write in his autobiography *The Street of Disillusion*:

> For weeks Madeline (sic) McLoughlin and I, as paid and skilled journalists, had the tough task of keeping away the opposition reporters and photographers. The opposition never allowed us a day or a night free from anxiety.
>
> My long experience of the Old Bailey made me realise that the task of taking Mr and Mrs Craig, and their daughter, Lucy, to that great Court of Justice every day ... without allowing even a 'Yes' or 'No' for quotes to the opposition was a formidable one.

He claimed that he had succeeded and added the incredibly callous observation: 'The ordeal was almost as mentally shattering for us as it was for the tragic Craig family.'

I doubt whether Mrs Craig would have shared his views. As she stood on the pavement outside the public entrance to the Old Bailey, her eyes were rimmed with red as if she had never stopped crying. Eventually, Harry Proctor snapped, 'That's enough,' and swept his charges up the steps into the court.

There was a long line of people standing in queues waiting to be let into the public gallery. Some had been there, it was said, all night in bitter cold. But the spivs, of whom there were hordes in Britain at that time, also meant business. Tickets were being issued for the trial in Court 2, as if for a theatre, with separate 'houses' for morning and afternoon sessions. The spivs had engaged down-and-outs to stand in the queues and were selling tickets for £30 to the punters. 'The Trial of the Century', as journalists were already calling it, was about to commence.

Happily none of the photographers present knew who I was, so I was able to struggle with my red bag and briefcase up the separate entrance to the barristers' robing room.

*

The robing room was crowded and it was with difficulty that I found a corner of the table for my wig box and began to robe. There was the chill, resentful hostility shown to all foreigners by the Old Bailey Bar Mess. I was made to feel an unwelcome intruder: a predator who was taking the bread out of their mouths.

The previous Wednesday, when I walked into the Bar robing room, I was just in time to hear Christmas Humphreys say in a tone of contempt, 'Oh, he's some young chap who's not been called long. I suppose he's got the brief because he's some relation of the Croydon solicitors.'

There was indeed in Croydon in those days a firm of solicitors called Parris, Milner & Co, but so far as I know I was not related in any way to the Parris of that firm, if there were one, and certainly I never in the whole of my professional life had a brief from them.

In theory, with a few exceptions, any practising barrister was in those days entitled to appear for a client in any court in England or Wales from the humblest magistrates' court to the highest court in the land, the Judicial Committee of the House of Lords. In practice there were more restrictive practices than those alleged to exist among the bummarees in the old fish market in Billingsgate.

7. The Trial

The country was divided into circuits, and a barrister could not appear for a client in another circuit without a member of that circuit being also employed. I was once 'circuit junior' at the Wakefield Quarter Sessions to Rose Heilbronn, who was not on the North Eastern but the Northern Circuit. All I did for my fee was to say 'Good morning' to her and, because she was a woman, help her on with her gown. I was fully engaged in the court next door to hers and never saw her again. Her case had finished before mine had.

In addition to those formal rules, various other stratagems were adopted by barristers and their clerks. I gave up going to Newcastle and Durham Assizes because it was carefully arranged by the locals that I was kept hanging about for days before my cases came on. A similar procedure applied on the one occasion on which I, a common law man, accepted a brief in the Chancery Division.

In the same way the Old Bailey Bar Mess made it very plain that they did not welcome trespassers from the North Eastern Circuit.

*

At ten-thirty the doors opened, and Lord Goddard took his seat in court to obsequious bows from counsel.

Craig, still in plaster, stood in the dock beside Bentley. He was now wearing a new sports jacket of modest shade and dark grey flannels, not the garish film-gangster garments in which I had seen him in prison. He had heeded my advice, although I fear that after the trial he was never to wear them again.

The clothes a person wears often have a profound effect on a jury, as, apparently, they do on electors. The advent of television in the House of Commons has resulted in the Labour opposition front bench turning up in suits and ties just like the grey men in grey suits opposite.

In one case I was involved in a couple were charged with stealing from under a bed in a Leeds lodging house a suitcase full of thousands of pounds in notes – which itself had been previously stolen. Another counsel appeared for the man, and I appeared for his mistress who had gladly helped him spend them. He was in prison but she had been granted bail. When I saw her she was wearing a lot of make-up and extravagant clothes. I told her to appear for the trial without make-up and wearing a plain white blouse and navy blue suit. She turned up looking as innocent and fresh as a dew drop. She was acquitted of all charges, both stealing and receiving stolen property, even though her boy-friend when in the witness box said it was she who had discovered the suitcase in another lodger's room and stolen it. Had she appeared as I first saw her, I'm sure the jury would have convicted her.

*

The charge was put to the accused by the clerk of the court.

> Christopher Craig, Derek William Bentley, you are charged that on the 2nd day of November last you murdered Sidney George Miles. Christopher Craig, are you guilty or not guilty?
> Not guilty.
> Derek William Bentley, are you guilty or not guilty?
> Not guilty.

The Lord Chief Justice then said, 'Craig may sit down.'
The courtesy of being seated, invariably extended to prisoners in all trials lasting more than a few minutes, was not extended to Bentley. He was kept standing by Goddard for two whole days and most of the third.
A jury of ten men and two women were placed in the jury box. As the first woman took the New Testament to be sworn, I stood up.
'I challenge that juror,' I said.

*

She was hustled out and replaced by a man. The same thing happened to the other woman. Lord Goddard looked irritably

92

7. *The Trial*

and ostentatiously at the clock, as if to suggest to the jury that I was wasting his and their time.

But I had good reasons for my challenge to the jury. In those days, before the breathalyser was introduced, almost every week I was engaged in defending clients charged with driving a motor car under the influence of drink. I had a pretty high success rate in that type of case. In fact there were only two cases I recall in which my client was convicted. One was a Commander Eden, a cousin of Anthony Eden, who had driven his Rolls-Royce off the road into the middle of a muddy field. He turned up at the North Riding Quarter Sessions for his trial wearing his Old Etonian tie, which gentlemanly Old Etonians only wear once a year. Presiding over the court was Judge Wrangham, also an Old Etonian.

I had one major difficulty already, because he was driving a Rolls-Royce. Juries, especially Yorkshire juries, would happily acquit a commercial traveller with a Morris Minor but were much more likely to convict the driver of a Rolls-Royce. On top of that there was his tie. I begged and prayed him not to go into the dock wearing it. I offered to lend him my own silver one but he would not hear of it.

Wrangham's summing up to the jury was the most vicious prosecution speech I had ever heard. My client was convicted, had his driving licence suspended for three years, was fined £250 and given three months' imprisonment. That, I reckon, was £250 for driving under the influence of drink, and three months for wearing an Old Etonian tie in the dock.

In such cases, in those days when defending counsel had an unlimited number of challenges to the jury, I always saw that I evicted all woman jurors from the jury. I thought that women were more likely to be total abstainers or Methodists, whereas most men were likely to share the sentiments of Mr Justice Stable, who when I remarked on the three-month sentence – a remarkably light one – he had imposed for a motor manslaughter, explained: 'I've driven a car often myself when I've been pissed as hell.'

In some cases I liked a lot of women on the jury – they were particularly useful in rape cases, where their sentiment invariably was: 'Well, she got what she asked for.' In this case I didn't want any women on because I thought they would identify with Mrs Miles, the widow of the murdered police officer. Later Frank Cassels told David Yallop that he thought my removal of them was unwise. He apparently believed that they would have identified with the mothers of Craig and Bentley. He may well have been right. But where there is a crime of violence, women become so blinded by their own fears and horror of it, that even if they entertain doubts about the defendant's guilt they are more likely to resolve their doubts in favour of the prosecution. With more vivid imaginations than men, they can see and feel it happening to them, and I felt sure that their minds in this case would have been with the widow of PC Miles. Mine was. I was sure theirs would have been.

Mrs Miles had been awarded a pension of £2 16s a week for the loss of her husband. Later, I was so outraged at this trifling sum that I got Bill Richardson (now Sir William) with whom I had shared many a bottle of good claret in the wine cellar near Gray's Inn and who was editor of *Reynolds News*, to get one of his staff, an ex-policeman, to write a piece about it. It had no influence, of course, on the mind of the government but it did raise a considerable sum for Mrs Miles.

*

But I had another reason for challenging the women jurors. I was a great believer in court-room psychology and thought it always important for defence counsel to make an impact – any sort of impact – on the jury. If he has a startling cross-examination to conduct, the moment can be delayed until then; if he has not, then some occasion has to be created to let the jury know that he exists. Besides, an intervention, whether it be a challenge to the indictment or to a juror, drives out of prosecuting counsel's head all those telling phrases he has prepared in order to create an indelible impression of guilt by his opening speech. It is surprising how all the punch can go out of the opening speech of even the most experienced prosecutor if his train of thought can be diverted in such a fashion. It is even better, of course, if one can find an excuse to interrupt prosecuting counsel in the course of his speech.

A trial is not only a conflict of facts; it is a clash of personalities. One personality, the judge or one of the counsel, will dominate. He will determine the atmosphere of the trial. It is for this reason that some counsel resort to gimmicks – such as snuff-taking, coloured cough mixture, or blatantly doing the *Times* crossword puzzle. Even an ordinary pair of horn-rimmed spectacles will do if put off and on sufficiently often.

'Khaki' Roberts, a great defence counsel, always appeared late in court, leaving his junior to cover the preliminaries. He had his clerk come in with great solemnity and place a big white brief tied with red tape on his place. He would then make a majestic appearance, like the celebrant at a choral communion service, and bow solemnly to the judge. During the prosecuting counsel's opening speech he would use an apparatus to blow something up his nostril while the jury looked on fascinated, ignoring the prosecutor's opening.

*

Christmas Humphreys made sure to include early in his opening speech for the prosecution a phrase which would bring him headlines in the evening papers. He got them. This time he said:

'The case for the prosecution is this: that Craig deliberately and wilfully murdered that police constable and thereafter gloried in the murder; that Bentley incited Craig to begin the shooting and, although technically under arrest at the actual time of the killing of Miles, was party to that murder and equally responsible in law.'

There were three evening newspapers in London in those days. All three carried virtually the same headline:

CRAIG GLORIED IN MURDER

Humphreys told the jury that what took place that night took place when there was a moon but it was generally obscured by clouds and for the most part the police were using torches.

Therefore what took place happened in circumstances in which 'there was either a fitful gleam or darkness'.

According to him, after he had been seized by Fairfax on the roof 'Bentley got away and shouted an observation, heard by three separate officers in the darkness in three separate places, which may be, in your view, the most important observation that Bentley made that night, "Let him have it, Chris." '

Humphreys repeated those words with emphasis: *'Let him have it, Chris.'* He went on:

> The immediate reply to that comment by Bentley was a loud report, and Fairfax was hit on the shoulder with what turned out to be a bullet from the gun which Craig held.
>
> That observation was not only heard by Sergeant Fairfax grappling with two men in the dark on the roof, but by another officer, McDonald, who was at that moment climbing up the same stack-pipe and by another officer who had arrived from an entirely different direction and who was further away to the right of your plan on the flat roof, PC Harrison.
>
> All three heard it, and all three heard the shot which followed immediately upon it.
>
> That statement, in the submission of the Prosecution, was a deliberate incitement to Craig to murder Sergeant Fairfax.
>
> It was spoken to a man whom he, Bentley, clearly knew had a gun. That shot began a gun fight in the course of which Miles was killed; that incitement, in the submission of the Prosecution, covered the whole of the shooting thereafter; even though at the time of the actual shot which killed PC Miles Bentley was in custody and under arrest.

The last sentence was an interesting comment, in the light of the judgment of the Court of Criminal Appeal on Bentley's case.

Humphreys told the jury that at least nine shots had been fired and made the point that, since the revolver only held six, this meant that Craig must have re-loaded. He concluded:

7. *The Trial*

The case for the Crown is this and nothing less, that Craig deliberately murdered PC Miles and, as I have said, thereafter gloried in the murder and only regretted he had not shot more. Bentley incited Craig to begin the shooting and, although he was technically under arrest at the time of the actual murder of PC Miles, was nevertheless still mentally supporting Craig in all that Craig continued to do; and in English law, and you may think in common sense, was in every sense party to that murder.

*

The first evidence was that of the two police officers who had made plans and photographs of the premises. But the next witness was Christopher Craig's father, Niven Matthews Craig. He was called by the prosecution merely to prove that his son was born on 19 May 1936. This gave me the opportunity to present an entirely different picture of Christopher Craig from that presented by the prosecution and, more importantly, by the newspapers who would undoubtedly have influenced the mind of the jury.

I think he went to Norbury Secondary Modern School until he was 15, did he not?

Yes.

But in spite of that, he never managed to read or write?

No; he suffered from what, I believe, is known as word blindness.

Word blindness. You tried, did you not, night after night, to teach him to read?

Oh, I did indeed, sir.

I think the only books he knows anything about are the books of Enid Blyton that he gets other people to read to him?

Yes.

I brought out his Army service in the 1914-1918 war as a Captain and in the Second World War and his own interest in weapons.

Was Christopher ever to your knowledge a violent boy?

Never; he was in fact quite the opposite.

Gentle?

Very gentle.

I think that until 18 months or 2 years ago he went regularly to a Bible Class at a church in Streatham?

He did; but, unfortunately, he did not wish to continue that, because he was very nervous of being asked to read a lesson and, as he could not read, that would have been a very embarrassing experience for him. For that reason he said he did not wish to continue to go to this Bible Class.

All his life he has been very conscious of the fact that he could not read, and was mocked by other boys for that reason?

Yes.

Humphreys must have thought that my cross-examination had had some effect, for he tried to discredit his own witness by suggesting that he had been convicted of having a gun without a licence in March 1952.

In fact it was March 1942, but Humphreys' interjection merely served to underline a point I was trying to make.

An intervention by Lord Goddard, undoubtedly intended to be hostile to Craig, merely helped to further the picture of Craig that I was trying to present to the jury. Humphreys said that Craig had been convicted at Hove Borough Juvenile Court in November 1951 for possession of an unlicensed firearm. Lord Goddard asked:

What was this boy doing at Hove at the time he was arrested? Was he on holiday or not?

No; he had just left school at that time and had started work in an engineering firm at Croydon, and the first duties he was given to perform were in the store-room, where he had to issue tools to the rest of the staff. Well, as he could not read or write the other members of the staff used to ridicule him and make fun of him because of his spelling, and he asked to leave this work. We asked him to carry on

98

for a little longer, but instead of carrying on he left home with his pay on a Friday night with a view to going over to France by boat from Brighton.

Well, he went off on a sort of frolic of his own?

That is why he was at Brighton.

*

The first important witness was Frederick Fairfax, at the time of the events a detective-constable in 'Z' Division of the Metropolitan Police but subsequently promoted to detective-sergeant, perhaps as a reward for his conduct that night, perhaps to give greater respectability to his evidence, and apparently transferred to 'C' Division. In his evidence in chief he said:

As we got to the corner of the stack, that is the bottom left-hand corner of the stack marked 'A' on the plan, Bentley broke away from me, and as he did so he shouted, 'Let him have it, Chris.' There was then a flash and a loud report, and I felt something strike my right shoulder which caused me to spin round and fall to the ground.

Just indicate to the jury on your body how the bullet went?

The bullet went through there [indicating].

At that time how far away were you from Craig?

About six feet.

What happened then?

As I was getting up from the ground, I saw one person moving away from me to my left, and one person moving to my right.

To get it clear; as a result of your being shot and knocked down, Bentley had got out of your grasp?

Yes.

What did you do when you saw one going left and one right?

I made a grab at the fellow on my right and found that I had again got a hold of the defendant Bentley. I struck him with my fist, and he fell to the ground. As he did so there was a second loud report, and I then pulled Bentley up in front of me as a shield.

Later in his evidence in chief he said that Bentley had broken away from him after the first shot had been fired and as a result of his being knocked down. That piece has been deleted from the edited version of the trial, but there is reference to it in the cross-examination of Frank Cassels.

You see what I am suggesting in this; that when that shot was fired you were not directly facing Craig?

Yes; we were actually diagonally with him; because we were approximately at the bottom left-hand corner of the stack and Craig was half left of me, and I was then pulling Bentley by his left arm.

Now are you saying, Sergeant Fairfax, that Bentley broke away before the shot was fired or after?

Definitely before the shot.

Then you were not holding him when the shot was fired?

No.

You see, I do not want to take advantage of any slip; but you did agree with my learned friend Mr Humphreys that Bentley broke away *after* the shot was fired; you said 'Yes' to the question he asked?

If I did I have made a mistake, because Bentley actually broke away from me before the shot was fired.

Lord Goddard rushed to the defence of the officer:

The witness is quite right; I have a note of it. 'As we got to the bottom of the left-hand corner Bentley broke away and shouted, 'Let him have it, Chris.' There was a shot, a flash and I felt something strike me.'

All Frank could do to exploit this evident contradiction was to say:

I quite agree, my lord; but subsequently Mr Humphreys asked a question which was framed like this: 'As a result of your being shot and knocked down did Bentley break away?', and the answer was 'Yes'. That is why I do not want to take advantage of it if it is a mistake.

In his evidence in chief Fairfax referred only to three shots having been fired by Craig: the first the one that hit him, the second after he had struck Bentley and the third the fatal shot that had killed Miles; and that was in accordance with his evidence recorded in the depositions. However, under cross-examination he said there had been about 10 shots fired (see Chapter 11 below).

*

Fairfax concluded his evidence in time for the luncheon break and the two accused were taken down from the dock. As I prepared to go out, a prison warder still in the dock beckoned me over, grinning all over his face.

'Do you know what your client has just said to me? – "I ought to have killed that fucker as well".'

It was just as well that the jury did not hear it.

*

The next prosecution witness was James Christie McDonald – as unhappy and shifty a witness as I ever saw. His story was that he had got over the expanding metal gate and had climbed up the vent pipe to within six feet of the top of it when he heard somebody shout 'Let him have it, Chris'.

The Lord Chief Justice intervened to ask:

Were you then on the ground, or were you still on the pipe?

I was practically level with the roof, my lord, but I could not get up the last six feet.

It was while you were still clinging to the pipe that you heard it?

Yes.

He was asked by Bass, junior counsel for the prosecution:

You heard someone shout, 'Let him have it, Chris.' I do not suppose you knew the voice at that time, did you?
    I did not.
    Have you heard the same voice since?
    I could not say for certain.
    Did you then come down the pipe?
    Yes.
    And did you hear something?
    Yes; I had reached the ground and I heard two or three shots fired from the direction of the roof.
    Did you then get up the pipe again?
    I did.

He was obviously unwilling to identify Bentley as the one who spoke the critical words, as he made plain while he was being cross-examined by Cassels:

Did you hear anything else said on the roof apart from this remark?
    I could not make out any more of the conversation; there was conversation, but I could not make out what it was.
    You just did hear this particular remark?
    Yes.
    I am suggesting you never heard that remark used by Bentley, or used by anybody else?
    I could not say whether it was Bentley who used it or not.

That did not please the judge. He asked irritably:

Well, did you hear the word 'Chris' used?
    I did.
    So far as you know, there were three people on the roof?
    Yes.
    There was Sergeant Fairfax and the two men?
    Yes.
    And you heard: 'Let him have it, Chris'; is that right?

That is right, my lord.

Very good.

McDonald's evidence did not accord with that of Fairfax who had sworn that the words 'Let him have it, Chris' were followed *immediately* by a shot from Craig. According to McDonald, he had reached the ground again before he heard two or three shots on the roof.

Frank was exposing this discrepancy in cross-examination:

Now, after you had heard that remark you heard some shots?

Some little time. I was on the ground before I heard the shots.

There was sufficient time between that remark and the first shot for you to have climbed down the drain-pipe and have reached the ground; is that right?

That is right.

That was a very valid point in favour of the defence, so in re-examination Bass asked:

Can you give me some idea as to how long it took you to get down the drain-pipe after you had heard the remark, 'Let him have it, Chris', before you heard the shot?

Not very long. The top foothold of the drain-pipe was sloping down, the two pipes coming out of the main pipe were sloping away, and once I got my feet in that I was down very quickly.

Was it minutes or seconds?

Minutes.

That answer did not please Lord Goddard and he exclaimed angrily: 'Minutes!'

To which the witness, plainly terrified, replied: 'Well, a minute, my lord.'

But even that didn't satisfy the judge:

103

What had you got to do?

I had to find my foothold as I went down, but it was not long.

Do you think you could have counted sixty?

I am not sure that I could.

'People can always say minutes when they mean seconds in these cases,' the judge commented.

Even that did not accord with Fairfax's evidence that use of the alleged words and the shot were *practically simultaneous*. And McDonald initially swore that he was clinging to the pipe when he first heard the words but later that he was on the ground.

*

The next witness to say that he heard Bentley use the words 'Let him have it, Chris' was PC Norman Harrison. Comment has already been made on his extraordinary agility in going round to the back of the premises, over a fence, on to the roof of the factory at No. 25 Tamworth Road, down again to the ground, into the garden of No. 26, through the house, back into Tamworth Road to the front of the factory, back again somehow into the garden of No. 26, up on to the factory roof and then along it to near the chimney stack. His ability to see everything that happened from there, a distance of over sixty feet from the lift shaft on a night so dark that Fairfax could not see the two youths until he was upon the roof, with the lift shaft obstructing his line of vision, was equally remarkable. As was his sense of timing. He claimed he was there before Fairfax got on to the roof and both saw and heard everything that happened. In cross-examination, he claimed he saw Fairfax actually climb on to the roof up the vent pipe although his line of vision from the chimney stack was obstructed both by the four roof lights and by the stair head.

He was absolutely positive, he said in cross-examination, that he had heard the words used by Bentley.

7. The Trial

*

The specialist who examined Christopher Craig after his dive from the roof top was called to describe his injuries. He conceded that Craig must have been in considerable pain. Lord Goddard objected when I began asking questions about the drugs administered and, at my request, the medical officer at Croydon General Hospital was called by the prosecution to produce evidence of drugs given to him in hospital, which included pentathol and pethadrine. I hoped to establish that if he had said the things attributed to him in hospital he was not in a proper frame of mind. Unhappily Craig was unable to give me any instructions about their alleged remarks because, he said, he had been concussed and unconscious for considerable periods of time.

*

Sergeant Stanley Shepherd gave evidence about various matters but more particularly about the statement alleged to have been made by Bentley.

In cross-examination Frank Cassels asked:

Now, do you say that this statement was taken completely at Bentley's dictation?
Yes.
Were any questions of any sort asked either by you or by Inspector Smith?
I asked no questions at all. Inspector Smith did say something about the date, and I wrote that date down – the 2 November.
Did Inspector Smith ask any questions whilst this statement was being taken?
No.
While you were writing down this statement were you repeating what you were writing?
Yes, occasionally.
All the time, or only occasionally?

I think that he hesitated a lot and I repeated what I had just written down.

Did not you or Inspector Smith at certain stages ask questions of him?

No.

Detective Chief Inspector John Leslie Smith gave evidence to similar intent. As has been indicated earlier, not even the prosecution believed them.

*

Lewis Charles Nickolls, Master of Science, a Fellow of the Royal Institute of Chemistry and Director of the Metropolitan Police Laboratory at New Scotland Yard, was called by the prosecution to talk about Craig's revolver. I had met him before when he had been Director of the Police Forensic Science Laboratory at Harrogate and did not think highly of his talents or his integrity. In my view he would say anything the police wanted him to say and would co-operate with them in fabricating evidence against an accused.

However, since he knew next to nothing about ballistics and he and I had clashed before in cases, often to his discomfort, he was prepared to accept almost anything that I, briefed by Major Chivers, a ballistics expert, was prepared to put to him. Had he not I would have been prepared to call Chivers; he was present in court. Nickolls readily agreed that Craig's sawn-off revolver would be inaccurate to the degree of 6 feet at a range of 39 feet; that the ammunition Craig had used was of lower calibre than required for the Eley .455 and it would therefore make it, in his own words, 'completely inaccurate'; that tommy gun .45 ammunition filed down to fit a .455 would sink further into the barrel and that an undersized bullet would result in wobbling in the rifling.

In fact I made so much progress with Nickolls in establishing that Craig's weapon was far too inaccurate for him to have any hope of hitting anybody he aimed at, especially since cutting it

down had removed both the sights and part of the rifling, that
Lord Goddard felt it necessary to intervene once again to bolster
up the prosecution's case. He asked Nickolls:

> This revolver, if it is fired off, and even if it is fired
> indiscriminately, is quite capable of killing people?
> Yes, it is capable of being lethal.
> No matter whether it is accurate or inaccurate?

He then addressed Christmas Humphreys:

> Mr Humphreys, this is a case in which an officer of justice
> was murdered – er – shot.
> Yes, my lord.
> Very different considerations, as you know, apply where
> an officer of justice in the course of the execution of his duty
> is killed.
> Yes, my lord; but, with great respect, I was following up
> with this witness what I imagine to be – I may be wrong –
> the opening to a certain line of defence.
> Well, if that defence is run I shall tell the jury that this is
> no defence at all.
> If your lordship pleases. My lord, that is the case for the
> Prosecution.

Goddard used the word 'murdered' in the hearing of the jury –
which was the very issue the jury were empanelled to decide. In
the corrected printed version, he added the word 'shot' as if
correcting his error. And he made it plain that his intention was
to tell the jury that my defence was no defence at all. Again, all
that was said in front of the jury.

*

By the rules of procedure I had to put Craig in the witness box
without opening my case to the jury, since I proposed to call no
other witnesses in order to be able to address the jury after the
final prosecution speech. In that the prosecution have an unfair

107

advantage. They can open their case to the jury, often in extravagant and damning terms, leaving those juries who had minds like Lord Goddard's with an indelible impression of guilt. Then they get a second speech. The advocate who calls only his client gets only one speech.

I thought Craig gave his evidence well, in spite of constant hostile interruptions by Goddard. He was, as I had urged him to be, candid and honest and Goddard's interruptions were designed to frustrate the case I was trying to build up. Typical was:

Did you know that firearms could kill people?
Yes, sir.
Let us get on to something that matters.

Craig claimed that he had fired on the ground a few feet in front of him to frighten Fairfax off. He said he never had any intention at any time of killing or doing harm to any officer. All he wanted to do was to frighten them away.

The judge came in again then with a prejudicial question:

Have you ever expressed any regret or sorrow that you killed that officer?
Yes, sir.
When?
When I am in prison, sir.

Another highly prejudicial question from the judge was:

The police had arrested your brother, had not they?
Yes, sir.
And he had been convicted?
Yes, sir.
And he had a gun?
Yes, sir.

No evidence had been adduced in the case about this. This was guilt by brotherhood – really putting the poison in for Craig.

Craig when he was cross-examined was firm in his denial that

Bentley ever said 'Let him have it, Chris'. In cross-examination by Humphreys reference was made to the evidence of Fairfax:

He has told us he came and grabbed Bentley, and while you were all there together by the head of that lift shaft you deliberately shot him?
I did not, sir.
Having been incited to do so by Bentley saying, 'Let him have it, Chris'. Are you saying you did not hear that?
Bentley did not say it, sir.
Three officers heard it in the darkness from different points of the compass. Are you saying he did not say it?
I am saying I did not hear it, and if they heard it they have better hearing than mine.

When Craig said he was hardly conscious in hospital half the time, Lord Goddard interjected the comment: 'Hardly conscious! Don't talk such nonsense.'

*

Frank Cassels then called Bentley.
It is pointless to go through the evidence he gave, but two eye witnesses have made comments on his performance in the witness box: Reginald Paget QC MP said in *Hanged and Innocent*, 'It would not be correct to say that Bentley made a fool of himself in the witness box – God had already done that for Bentley.' Arthur Smith, Goddard's clerk, commented in his memoirs about Goddard: 'Bentley emerged from these proceedings as little more than a kind of zombie.'

*

When the lunch-time break on Wednesday arrived Arthur Smith came to tell us that Lord Goddard intended to sit to finish that evening.
The jury were sent out early to lunch while the three counsel were engaged in legal argument. Goddard addressed me when

109

they had gone. He was not disposed to leave the issue of murder or manslaughter to the jury. He intended to direct them that, on the evidence, they could only find a verdict of murder. He addressed me:

> Mr Parris, the murdered man in this case was a police officer. If, therefore, the jury are of opinion (and I do not see how they can be otherwise in view of your own client's evidence) that Craig knew they were police, and as he fired a revolver, what does intention matter in the case of a police officer? It has been the law for centuries, has not it?

I advanced the argument that only when the prisoner used violence against a police officer 'with intent to inflict grievous bodily injury' was he guilty of murder, but if in the course of the struggle 'he accidentally caused an injury, it would be manslaughter', relying upon the judgment of Mr Justice Brett in *R* v. *Porter* 12 Cox's Criminal Cases 444 and *R* v. *Appleby* 1940 Cohen's Criminal Appeal Reports. There was much legal argument going back to Hale and Foster, in the course of which I advanced the proposition, that if it were an accidental *injury*, it would be manslaughter. Goddard said:

> I say I am quite prepared to accept that if it is an accidental injury. The question is what is accidental? I cannot say an injury is accidental when a man is firing, even if he says, 'I did not intend to fire at the man, but in another direction.' He is doing a deliberate act.
>
> But it must be the injury which is accidental. He accidentally causes an injury – not the act.
>
> I think that is a little too subtle for me.

It would be boring to repeat the arguments, but I still think I was right legally. A deliberate act which causes an accidental, that is an unintended, injury – the death of a policeman – is only manslaughter, but an act done with intent to cause injury is murder. I do not suggest it is the law now, especially after the disgraceful case of *DPP* v. *Smith* was decided in the House of

Lords in 1960 by a Bench of which Lord Goddard, then retired, was one. In that case again a police officer had been killed and the Court of Criminal Appeal had substituted a verdict of manslaughter for that of murder. They relied upon the 1947 case of *R v. Steane*, a judgment by Lord Goddard, of which I was, I regret to say, ignorant. It would have given me great pleasure to have quoted it to his face, and to the jury.

In that judgment, the Lord Chief Justice had said:

No doubt if the prosecution prove an act the natural consequences of which would be a certain result and no evidence or explanation is given, then a jury may, on a proper direction, find that the prisoner is guilty of doing the act with the intent alleged. But if on the totality of the evidence there is room for more than one view as to the intent of the prisoner, the jury should be directed that it is for the prosecution, and if, on a review of the whole evidence, they either think the intent did not exist, or they are left in doubt as to the intent, the prisoner is entitled to be acquitted.

The Court of Criminal Appeal had quashed Smith's conviction for murder, but the Director of Public Prosecutions, Sir Theobald Matthews, did not agree and took the case to the House of Lords, which overruled the Court of Criminal Appeal. However, the judgment in the Smith case was reversed by section 8 of the Criminal Justice Act of 1967.

None the less, with what authorities I had, I managed to persuade Goddard to leave the question of murder or manslaughter to the jury. It was a considerable success because earlier in the case he was proposing to tell the jury that my defence for Craig was no defence.

As to Bentley, Goddard summarised the position accurately: 'He must be aware that Craig was armed and the jury must be satisfied that he intended with Craig to offer violent resistance.'

*

Christmas Humphreys made his closing speech for the prosecution.

However, when I came to outline to the jury what I claimed was the law – which by leaving the decision of murder or manslaughter to the jury, Goddard had already accepted – he interrupted me in my final moments:

> Mr Parris, I think it is only right I should tell the jury that what you are saying to them now – no doubt with the best intentions – is not the law. If all your hypotheses were right, the defence of accident is not open to him, for the reason I shall explain to the jury, and it would be murder.
>
> My lord, the Defence base it on the case of *Appleby*.
>
> You have misread it.
>
> 'If in the course of a struggle, he accidentally caused an injury ...'
>
> A man does not accidentally cause an injury if he shoots. The act has got to be accidental.
>
> As I understand it, it was the injury which has to be accidental.

It was, of course, devastatingly destructive of all my arguments.

Frank Cassels made his speech for Bentley.

The Lord Chief Justice must have thought our speeches had too much influence on the jury. Although he had indicated to us his intention to 'sit to finish' he adjourned the court until the next day. It was only shortly after three o'clock.

He wanted a clear field for his own summing up.

*

So at 10.30 am on Thursday, 11 December 1952, Lord Goddard began his charge to the jury. It was, as all his charges to juries were, not an impartial summing up of the evidence but a vicious speech for the prosecution.

He began by saying:

7. The Trial

Now, members of the jury, this is in many respects a terrible case.

The two accused go out, on a shop breaking expedition, armed with a service revolver, a dreadful weapon in the shape of a knuckleduster and two knives which may or may not be described as daggers.

Now let us put out of our minds in this case any question of films or comics, or literature of that sort. These things are always prayed in aid nowadays when young persons are in the dock, but they have really very little to do with the case. These two young men, or boys, whatever you like to call them, are both of an age which makes them responsible to the law – they are over 14 – and it is surely idle to pretend in these days that a boy of 16 does not know the wickedness of taking out a revolver of that description and a pocketful of ammunition and firing it when he is on an unlawful expedition and the police are approaching him. You will remember that so far as Craig is concerned, by his own words he supplied a motive for what he was doing, for he said that he hated the police because they had got his brother 12 years – which seems to show that his brother was convicted for a very serious offence to receive a sentence of that length.

That, of course, was a nasty smear of Craig by relationship. Goddard failed to mention that it was the allegation of police officers alone and that Craig and Bentley had both denied that Craig had ever used those words. He deliberately savaged my defence of Craig by saying:

Gentlemen, there is another and further consideration in this case to which I want to direct your particular attention. Miles, the dead man, was a police officer, and the law for centuries – in fact, ever since there has been law in this country – has given special protection to police officers while in the execution of their duty, or perhaps it is more accurate to say that in the case of the killing of a peace officer – I use the expression 'peace officer' which is the old

113

expression in English law for the modern police constable –
he is in exactly the same position as the old parish
constables were before there was any regular police force,
and who were the only peace officers in the country – in the
case of a peace officer who is killed, the law does not give the
accused the same defences as in the case of other persons; it
takes one away, and I am going to direct you that this is the
law: 'If a police officer has arrested, or is endeavouring to
arrest (and that includes coming on the scene for the
purpose of arresting) a person, and the arrest, if affected,
would be lawful, and that person, for the purpose of
escaping, or of preventing or hindering the arrest, does a
wilful – that is to say, an intentional – act which causes the
death of the officer, he is guilty of murder, whether or not
he intended to kill or do grievous bodily harm.'

Now you will bear that in mind – and I will read it to you
again: 'If a police officer has arrested, or is endeavouring to
arrest (which includes coming on to the scene for the
purpose of arresting) a person, and the arrest, if effected,
would be lawful, and that person for the purpose of
escaping, or of preventing or hindering the arrest, does a
wilful act which causes the death of the officer, he is guilty
of murder, whether or not he intended to kill or to do
grievous bodily harm.'

In that case the only possible way of reducing the crime to
manslaughter is to show that the act was accidental, and
not wilful.

He went on in the same vein, and then said:

Now, was it a wilful act which caused the injury? As I told
you, the question is not whether the result was accidental
in the sense that more harm was caused than was intended.
A person who is doing such things as firing off a revolver at
police officers cannot say: 'Well, it was an accident that I
killed him, because I never intended to kill him.' The
answer is: 'You were doing a deliberate act, a wilful act.'

Now that I have explained the law to you, it may be that

you will have some difficulty, as I do not hesitate to say I have, in understanding what defence there can be in the case of the prisoner Craig. There he was on this roof, armed. His revolver was loaded. When he took it there he had spare ammunition from which at some time he reloaded it, and you heard, too, that some of this ammunition had been specially filed down to fit the revolver. There he was on the roof with a loaded revolver, firing off shots until his revolver was empty, and then he reloaded the revolver and continued to fire, because, as you know, the revolver contains six chambers and he fired altogether nine shots, and two, I think, that were found that had not detonated; so in all he tried to fire eleven. If that is not a deliberate act, a deliberate firing, it is difficult to understand what would be. But you will remember, and you will bear in mind, that we are only concerned with the death of Police Constable Miles on this indictment, and PC Miles, you will remember, was killed by the third shot which this youth fired ...

The aiming does not seem to have been bad does it? Three shots, police officers hit, one fortunately slightly, the other hit between the eyes, so that blood gushed out and he fell dead instantaneously.

This, of course, was totally contrary to the evidence. He then went through the evidence and added:

Now, gentlemen of the jury, think of those facts together. Is it possible – if it is, you will always find a merciful verdict if you can – to say that that shooting was accidental? I have told you that you have got to find, before you can reduce this case to manslaughter, that the shooting was accidental, not that the result of the shooting was accidental – quite a different matter.

He then turned to the case against Bentley:

The first thing that you have got to consider is: Did Bentley know that Craig was armed? Now, you know, because I sit

115

on the Bench and you sit in the jury-box it is not necessary that we leave our common sense at home. The great virtue of trial by jury is that jurymen can exercise the common sense of ordinary people. Can you suppose for a moment, especially when you have heard Craig say that why he carried a revolver was for the purpose of boasting and making himself a big man, that he would not have told his pals he was out with that he had got a revolver? Is it not almost inconceivable that Craig would not have told him, and probably shown him the revolver which he had? That is quite apart from what Bentley said afterwards. I should think you would come to the conclusion that the first thing, almost, Craig would tell him, if they were going off on a shop-breaking expedition, was: 'It's all right. I've got a revolver with me.'

No witness had ever said that. It was pure speculation on the part of the Lord Chief Justice. He then went on:

Then see what Bentley had on him. Where is that knuckleduster? Apparently it was given to him by Craig, but Bentley was armed with this knuckleduster.

Have you ever seen a more horrible sort of weapon? You know, this is to hit a person in the face with who comes at you. You grasp it *here*, your fingers go through – I cannot quite get mine through, I think – and you have got a dreadful heavy steel bar to strike anybody with: and you can kill a person with this, of course.

Then did you ever see a more shocking thing than that?

You have got a spike with which you can jab anybody who comes at you; if the blow with the steel is not enough, you have got this spike at the side to jab. You can have it to see, if you like, when you go to your room.

It is a shocking weapon. Here was Craig armed with a revolver and that sheath-knife. Hand me that sheath-knife – the big one.

One wonders, really, what parents can be about in these days, allowing a boy of 16 – they say, perhaps, they do not know, but why do not they know? – to have a weapon like this which he takes about with him? It is not a new one, you can see: it is pretty well worn. That was the thing that Craig was taking about.

Where is the other knife? Here is Bentley with a smaller knife, but you can feel it is sharp and pointed. What is he carrying that with him for in his coat, not even with a sheath on it?

Can you believe it for a moment although Bentley has said he did not know Craig had the gun? You are not bound to believe Bentley if you think the inference and common sense of the matter is overwhelming that he must have known that he had it.

He then turned to the allegation that Bentley had used the words 'Let him have it, Chris' and said:

There is one thing I am sure I can say with the assent of all you twelve gentlemen, that the police officers that night, and those three officers in particular, showed the highest gallantry and resolution; they were conspicuously brave. Are you going to say they are conspicuous liars? – because if their evidence is untrue that Bentley called out, 'Let him have it, Chris', those three officers are doing their best to swear away the life of that boy. If it is true, it is, of course, the most deadly piece of evidence against him. Do you believe that those three officers have come into the box and sworn what is deliberately untrue? – those three officers who on that night showed a devotion to duty for which they are entitled to the thanks of the community?

This, of course, was a masterly *non sequitur*; bravery has nothing to do with truthfulness. It invited the jury to believe that if they found Craig guilty of manslaughter or acquitted Bentley they would be convicting three brave officers of perjury.

Goddard dismissed the case for Bentley in two sentences:

In the case of Bentley, Bentley's defence is: 'I didn't know he

117

had a gun, and I deny that I said, "Let him have it, Chris." I never knew he was going to shoot, and I didn't think he would.'

Against that denial (which, of course, is the denial of a man in grievous peril) you will consider the evidence of the three police officers who have sworn to you positively that those words were said.

He ended his summing up with:

Gentlemen of the jury, I started by saying this was a terrible case. It is dreadful to think that two lads, one, at any rate, coming, and I dare say the other, from decent homes, should with arms of this sort go out in these days to carry out unlawful enterprises like warehouse-breaking and finish by shooting policemen.

You have a duty to the prisoners.

You will remember, I know, and realise, that you owe a duty to the community, and if young people, but not so young – they are responsible in law – commit crimes of this sort, it is right, quite independent of any question of punishment, that they should be convicted, and if you find grounds for convicting them, it is your duty to do so.

That is what appears in the edited transcript. What in fact he said was: 'Unless you can find grounds for not convicting them, it is your duty to do so.'

*

It was at that stage that I rose. I asked:

My lord, before the jury retire might I invite your lordship to correct one mis-statement of fact?

Certainly.

Your lordship said that Sergeant Fairfax said it was the third shot which was the fatal one. That would appear to be so from his deposition, but he said in evidence that it was the seventh or eighth. That appears in the cross-examination, my lord.

There was a discussion about what Fairfax had said, but Goddard eventually ended the discussion by saying: 'I do not know that it very much matters'; although in his summing up against Craig he had made the deadly point that his aim did not seem to be that bad.

Goddard turned to the jury:

Will you consider your verdict? Would you like any of these? Would you like the statement? I ought to remind you, but it does not really matter, because Bentley has been in the witness-box and really repeated his evidence on oath, that strictly speaking the written statement made is not evidence against Craig, but the evidence he has given in the witness-box is all part of the evidence in the case. Will you tell me, gentlemen, if you would like any of the Exhibits? Do you want any of the weapons?

At that stage, there was an extraordinary episode.

Half the jury had filed out, but one, who was later to be the foreman of the jury, said, 'My lord, I would like to see Sergeant Fairfax's coat and waistcoat.'

At that there was an extraordinary outburst of rage from Goddard. He screamed at the jury: 'You will remember you are not considering the wounding of Sergeant Fairfax.' He picked up the knuckleduster and smashed it into the desk before him. The damage is there to this day, I am told. 'You are considering the murder of a police officer.'

The edited version of the trial purports to record that he said:

'Yes. You will remember, of course, gentlemen, you are not considering the wounding of Sergeant Fairfax. You are considering the death of PC Miles.' But the words he actually used are those which I have recorded, which I wrote down in my notebook at the time and which were also noted by a young barrister, Anthony Samuelson, present in court at the time. He told Yallop, accurately: 'Lord Goddard lost control of himself.'

119

The dutiful jury retired at 11.15 am and returned at 12.30 pm to return a verdict of guilty against both Craig and Bentley, with a recommendation to mercy in Bentley's case.

*

Lord Goddard then passed sentence on Bentley, the black cap on his wig.

> Derek William Bentley, you are 19 years of age; it is my duty to pass upon you the only sentence which the law can pass for the crime of wilful murder. The sentence of the Court upon you is that you be taken from this place to a lawful prison, and thence to a place of execution, and there you suffer death by hanging, and that your body be buried within the precincts of the prison in which you shall have been last confined before your execution; and may the Lord have mercy upon your soul. Take him down.

The black cap was then removed by Arthur Smith, his clerk.

> Christopher Craig, you are under 19, but in my judgment and evidently in the judgment of the jury you are the more guilty of the two.
>
> Your heart was filled with hate, and you murdered a policeman without thought of his wife, his family, or himself; and never once have you expressed a word of sorrow for what you have done.
>
> I can only sentence you to be detained until Her Majesty's pleasure be known.
>
> I shall tell the Secretary of State when forwarding the recommendation of the jury in Bentley's case that in my opinion you are one of the most dangerous young criminals who has ever stood in that dock.
>
> While the jury were out considering their verdict in this case, I had to deal with another case in which you were concerned with another boy whom you led into it in holding up an elderly couple at the point of revolvers and stealing

from them; and it is quite obvious that the people in this country will not be safe if you are out of prison.

I shall recommend the time which I suggest to the Secretary of State that you shall be kept in confinement.

The sentence upon you is that you be kept in strict custody until the pleasure of Her Majesty be known.

Take him down.

8

Bentley's Appeal

Christopher Craig's solicitor, Nelson, who was nowhere to be seen during the trial, did not instruct me to enter an appeal on his behalf. Indeed, so far as I know he never saw his client himself, let alone discussed with him whether he wished to appeal. There is nothing that counsel can do if he is not instructed to act by solicitors, although I took the view that there was a legal case that the direction on law given by Goddard to the jury was totally wrong and should be considered not only by the Court of Appeal but, as a point of public importance, by the House of Lords.

Frank Cassels did appeal, however, on behalf of Bentley.

He came before a Court of Criminal Appeal consisting of Mr Justice Croom-Johnson, Mr Justice Ormerod and Mr Justice Pearson. The last two were reasonable men; the presiding judge was a bastard.

Frank told the court that there were two points of appeal. First:

That the learned judge failed adequately to put the Appellant's defence before the jury. As I said, this was a case that lasted some considerable time, and the only reference in his lordship's summing-up to the defence of this particular Appellant is contained on page 138E.

The paragraph first of all puts forward to the point referred to on behalf of Craig, and then in the middle of the paragraph there comes this sentence: 'In the case of Bentley, Bentley's defence is: "I didn't know he had a gun,

123

and I deny that I said 'Let him have it, Chris'. I never knew he was going to shoot, and I didn't think he would." ' That was the only reference to the defence of this Appellant.

He pressed on with his appeal, despite constant barracking from Croom-Johnson, including:

All this was matter for the jury, was not it, including the fact that, according to one witness at least, if the jury chose to accept his evidence, this prisoner had said what kind of gun it was Craig was carrying?

Frank replied:

With respect, I entirely agree that all that was matter for the jury to consider. What I say is this, that when a learned judge presiding at a trial of this description is putting the facts that the jury should consider, he should, if he refers to the Prosecution's evidence with regard to a specific incident, if there is a denial by the Defendant that the incident has ever taken place he should put both sides of that particular issue before the jury.

There was considerable discussion between Croom-Johnson and Frank Cassels about what a judge needed to tell a jury about a defendant's case.

Having clearly lost on that point, Frank then moved on to his other claim: that even if there had been evidence of a joint venture to resist arrest, at some stage that must come to an end. In the course of argument on this point one of Croom-Johnson's interjections was:

That may turn – I do not say it does and do not be lulled into a false sense of security – upon what the joint adventure was; were they arming themselves, or was one of them arming himself, with the knowledge of the other, on the basis that they were to resist arrest if apprehended or interrupted in their joint adventure? If that is the right view, it may be that the fact that one of them has been arrested does not prevent the matter still being one in which the joint adventure is not over.

Frank replied:

With respect, that may well be right in this particular case. My complaint is that no suggestion of that sort was put before the jury during the course of the summing up.

Croom-Johnson came back:

A judge in the course of summing up a criminal trial cannot deal with every little point; the judge must be allowed a little latitude, mustn't he?

The question whether the joint venture (if there was one) had ended was not a 'little point'. Frank Cassels replied:

The point was made at an early stage of the trial that this man was under arrest at the time the fatal shot was fired. That matter was not put before the jury, and therefore, so far as one can know without retiring with the jury themselves, they gave no consideration to the question that this man at the time the fatal shot was fired, and for some considerable time before, was under arrest and being held by the police officer.

Christmas Humphreys in his reply contended that the conviction was safe, in the course of which he said:

What does matter is whether Bentley shouted in the first instance, 'Let him have it, Chris' – 'Let him have it, Chris' – because if he did, then you can consider whether that does not show, firstly, that he knew that 'Chris' had the revolver, and secondly, that he was calling upon 'Chris' to seek violence to prevent arrest. So the Chief Justice is virtually saying: 'The arrest point does not matter very much one

125

way or the other', and is certainly not putting it against Bentley. Unless your lordships have any further point, that is all I have to say.

Croom-Johnson:

You mean by that, that whether he was under arrest, he was still acting in the joint enterprise?

Humphreys:

That was the case for the Crown then and is today.

The judgment given by Croom-Johnson, dismissing the appeal, contained some surprising passages. He said that Bentley's defence was

> carefully put, adequately put and properly put by the Chief Justice and it was then up to the jury to decide 'Aye' or 'No': did they accept the prisoner's denials, or did they accept the evidence of two witnesses who spoke affirmatively to statements made by the Appellant and, I think, another witness who was not able to give the main evidence but did depose to hearing the words or similar words spoken by somebody.
>   In those circumstances, it seems to me that the matter was essentially a matter for the jury to decide, and I do not think I need say anything more about it. In the opinion of the Court, the idea that there was a failure on the part of the Chief Justice to say anything short of what was required in putting that sort of case to the jury is entirely wrong.

He then turned to the other point, that

> the Appellant could not be held responsible for the act because the joint enterprise was at an end.
>   That depends on what the jury thought was the joint enterprise.

8. Bentley's Appeal

If they thought it was an enterprise to go and murder somebody and that was over and done with so that the joint enterprise was finished, they might very well have taken that view.

I do not say it would have been the right view, but they might have taken the view that the enterprise was then finished as soon as one of them was arrested, but they might equally well have taken the view, and there was ample material for them to take it, and no complaint is made of the summing up with regard to this, that the enterprise was not merely a burglarious enterprise but an enterprise in which they were to secure themselves against the possibility of arrest by arming themselves against those who came to apprehend them.

In those circumstances the jury might very well have taken quite a different view as to whether the enterprise had finished or not.

It is a little difficult for Mr Cassels because his own client was asked specifically at the hearing whether he was under arrest at the time when this shot which killed Miles was fired.

He would not have it. He said he had not been arrested, that he was not under arrest, that the police officer had not detained him, and all the rest of it.

In the face of that it seems to us that it is idle to suggest that this point, if it be the point, about the arrest is one which the jury could take into consideration and about which the Chief Justice ought to have directed the jury.

The answers given in cross-examination by an individual on trial do sometimes have the result of destroying the possibility of a good point of law being persisted in which the learned counsel has endeavoured to get on its feet before a jury, and it seems to us that there is nothing in this point on either of the two grounds.

In our opinion this is nothing more than an ordinary appeal in a murder trial, an ordinary appeal which is, in our judgment, without foundation and which is accordingly dismissed.

127

The paragraph about being under arrest was an extraordinary perversion of Bentley's evidence. His evidence was that he had been arrested but was not being physically held all the time; that, too, was the evidence of the police officers.

This 'ordinary appeal' was over in about an hour. Bentley's fate now rested with the Home Secretary, Sir David Patrick Maxwell Fyfe.

Christopher Craig.

Derek Bentley.

The scene of the crime: Barlow & Parker's warehouse roof.

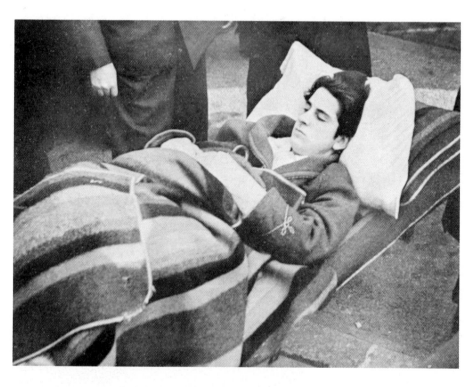

Christopher Craig at Croydon Magistrate's Court.

John Parris, counsel for Craig.

Frank Cassels, counsel for Bentley.

Christmas Humphreys, counsel for the Crown.

Rayner Goddard, Lord Chief Justice of England.

PC Sidney Miles, shot dead on Barlow & Parker's warehouse roof, 2 November 1952.

DCI John Smith.

DC Frederick Fairfax, PC James McDonald and PC Norman Harrison.

Mr and Mrs Craig leaving the Old Bailey during the trial.

Mr and Mrs Bentley and their daughter Iris visit Derek Bentley under sentence of death in Wandsworth Prison.

Sydney Silverman MP.

Sir David Maxwell Fyfe,
Home Secretary.

A crowd of demonstrators at the gates of Wandsworth Prison on 28 January 1953, as an official tries to post the notice of execution of Derek Bentley.

9

'The Nearest Thing to Death in Life'

David Maxwell Fyfe, later to become Lord Kilmuir, was, as one of his Prime Ministers, Harold Macmillan, described him in his memoirs, 'stupid'.

Another Prime Minister under whom he served, Churchill, had no higher opinion of him, as I found when later I was living near Menton and the former premier was occupying the penthouse apartment over the Hotel de Paris in Monte Carlo lent to him by Onassis. At the time I was working on a biography of Graham Sutherland, the artist, who lived near me and whom I saw almost every evening at dinner.

I was interested to see Churchill to get a direct quotation from him about what he thought of Sutherland's portrait of him. At its presentation in Westminster Hall, Churchill had referred with long-drawn-out, heavy sarcasm to 'this – interesting – example of – modern – art' and I thought that perhaps he might have been less polite and more candid with me. Graham was also curious to find out whether it still existed or whether, as was claimed, it had been burnt by Lady Churchill. By that time, as was often the case with the subjects of Graham's portraits, the artist and the subject were not on speaking terms.

I had several appointments to talk to Churchill. On some occasions he was completely gaga and didn't know who he was or who I was. In the evenings, he was lifted across in a chair from the Hotel de Paris to the Roulette Room in the Casino. There he would sit, throwing counters on the table, not conscious of what he was doing. On other occasions, when he had made an appointment to see me, usually about lunch time, he was totally

129

pissed, having drunk a bottle of Scotch that morning.

On one occasion, however, I found him entirely rational, friendly and witty. I could never get a straight answer out of Churchill as to whether the portrait had in fact been destroyed; so Graham may yet be proved right. And Churchill would not let me publish his feelings about it; but he did say to me, off the record, 'Dreadful! why he painted me without feet!' But our conversation before lunch strayed into other areas, including Maxwell Fyfe. He said to me:

'Of course, the man was a complete bloody fool. But he was a loyal and servile bloody fool. Every government needs people like that to keep it going.'

As to the execution of Derek Bentley, Churchill professed to know nothing whatsoever about it. He was, he said, on the Atlantic at the time, on the *Queen Mary* coming back from the States. He did not recall receiving a telegram from the Bentley family asking him to intervene, nor did he recall that forty-eight hours after the shooting of PC Miles he had demanded a special report from the police, supplied by Detective Inspector Smith. He had, he claimed, nothing whatever to do with the execution of Derek Bentley. It was a matter entirely for the Home Secretary.

*

The nearest thing to death in life
is David Patrick Maxwell Fyfe.

This couplet was written by Harry Hylton-Foster QC. It was a reference to Maxwell Fyfe's deathly pallor, but also to the fact that he was extremely stupid.

*

The public, who had been ready to lynch both Craig and Bentley at the time of the committal proceedings, now swung round when it became apparent that, although Craig could not be executed, it was likely that Bentley would be.

9. 'The Nearest Thing to Death in Life'

Letters arrived in their thousands at 1 Fairview Road, New-bury, the Bentleys' home. At one time there were 500 telephone calls a day. A reprieve petition was signed by 100,000 people. Stickers appeared on the bumpers of cars: 'Bentley must not die.' Bentley's father issued an appeal to the public:

We appeal to everyone in this country to give careful consideration to the following vital facts in the case of the State versus my son, Derek Bentley.

1. Derek had not been previously engaged in any crime of violence; he was not a hardened criminal; his only previous offence was a minor one for which he had paid.

2. On the night of the crime he was not armed.

3. If he acted in concert with Craig in the dastardly murder of PC Miles, why did he not make use of the knuckleduster to avoid being taken into custody?

4. At the time the shot was fired he was held by Sergeant Fairfax.

5. He did not have any reason to hold a grudge against the police, as did Craig.

6. The words: 'Let him have it, Chris', if said, could have meant, 'Let him have the gun.'

7. If he had not been taken into custody it is likely he might have deterred Craig from the act that has left my boy, and not Craig, in the shadow of the hangman's noose.

8. It has been argued by some that the law should be allowed to take its course in order to set an example to other wrong-doers, but in the name of British justice why pick on my boy, who has been guilty only of a technical offence?

131

On 22 January 1953 the Attorney General, Sir Lionel Heald, announced that he had refused to grant his fiat for an appeal to the House of Lords judicial committee, the highest court in the land. That was not entirely surprising to informed observers. Fiats are only granted when there is a point of law, and a point of law of *exceptional public importance*. There was no point of law in Bentley's case, still less one that could be applicable to other subsequent cases.

On the morning of 26 January 1953 a reporter came to the house in Fairview Road to enquire whether it was true that Maxwell Fyfe had refused an appeal. The Bentleys knew nothing of it, but when he left they began to search desperately through the post. So much had come that it had all been dumped in the bath until it could be sorted out.

Eventually they came across a brown envelope with OHMS on the outside. Mr Bentley tore it open; it read:

I am directed by the Secretary of State to inform you that he has given careful consideration to the petition submitted by you on behalf of your son, Derek Bentley, and I am to express to you his deep regret that after considering all the circumstances of the case he has failed to discover sufficient grounds to justify him in advising Her Majesty to interfere with the due course of law.

> I am Sir
> your obedient servant,
> F. A. Newman

Mrs Bentley and Iris Bentley collapsed with screams and had to be put under sedation by a doctor.

*

On the evening of that day Sydney Silverman, Labour MP for Nelson and Colne, presented a motion signed by fifty members of Parliament which called for the reprieve of Derek Bentley. Other members subsequently signed the motion and many more promised to support it. There is little doubt that it would have been carried on a free vote. But Mr Speaker Morrison ordered that it be removed from the Order Paper at ten o'clock that night.

When the house sat again the next day, 27 January, Sydney Silverman rose at three o'clock to question the Speaker's action in removing the motion from the Order Paper. He argued that 'Prerogative of Mercy' in this country is not an arbitrary act as it might be in some totalitarian states. It is as much subject to the constitutional principles of a Parliamentary democracy as any other act by any other person. He claimed that when a Minister of the Crown gave advice in any matter whatsoever, he was subject to the sovereignty and directions of the House.

The House was crowded and tense. Reg Paget, himself a barrister, supported Silverman. He said:

> We are a sovereign assembly. A three-quarter-witted boy of nineteen is to be hanged for a murder that he did not commit and which was committed fifteen minutes after he was arrested.
>
> Can we be made to keep silent when a thing as horrible and as shocking as this is to happen?

Leslie Hale in the same debate claimed that until 1916 it was commonplace to raise questions of ministers about the Royal Prerogative of Mercy and this power was taken away from the House 'because we were executing so many decent Irishmen'. It became, he claimed, 'a burden on Ministers to defend themselves at that time'. However, he conceded that when he himself had attempted in a similar fashion in 1947 to question the minister concerned in a capital case the Speaker had refused to accept his motion.

The current edition of Erskine May's *Parliamentary Practice* (1983) is categorical: 'In any case involving a capital sentence on which the exercise of the prerogative of Mercy depends it should not be made the subject of a question while the sentence is pending nor may the sentence itself be raised in a question while it is pending.' It quotes numerous rulings going back to 1887 for that proposition.

It should be recalled that the House of Commons has also refused to allow members to question ministers on other matters relating to the Royal Prerogative: about the award of honours, ecclesiastical patronage and the dissolution of Parliament.

It may well be a ridiculous situation that a minister cannot be challenged about the advice he gives to the sovereign about the exercise of the Royal Prerogative of Mercy until after the sentence has been carried out, but that is what the House of Commons itself has decided. After the execution, a minister can be criticised either in a vote on supply or in an adjournment debate or on a substantive motion.

*

Maxwell Fyfe was due that evening, 27 January, to be the guest of a Burns Club to propose 'the immortal memory'. He cancelled his appointment. 'I felt it was not the occasion to attempt a speech on a poet whose humorous poems formed a great part of his output and success,' he later wrote in his autobiography.

So he went home for dinner. He was then told that a deputation of Members of Parliament wished to see him, so he went back to the House. The deputation was led by Aneurin Bevan and included the former Solicitor-General, Lynn Ungoed-Thomas (later to become a High Court Judge), Reginald Paget QC and Sydney Silverman. They took with them a formal petition signed by 200 MPs which read:

> We, the undersigned members of the Commons House of Parliament, believing the advice tendered by you to Her Majesty the Queen in the case of Derek Bentley to be grievously mistaken and out of accord with the natural justice of the case, urge that even now you will advise Her Majesty to exercise the Royal Prerogative of Mercy so that the sentence of death on him be not executed.

Maxwell Fyfe listened to them in silence while Aneurin Bevan urged him to pay attention to public opinion.

9. 'The Nearest Thing to Death in Life'

*

That evening I was dining in my club, the National, in St James's with a friend, Ann Clark. She had wanted to talk to me about her matrimonial affairs. The National Club was very much a male affair, often compared to Hell because you could not get near the fire for bishops. There was a separate ladies' dining room in which members were allowed to entertain women guests. Ann and I had it to ourselves.

Ann was then an active supporter of Mrs Van der Elst, the eccentric wealthy woman who led a campaign for the abolition of the death penalty and who turned up in her yellow Rolls-Royce outside the prison gates whenever there was an execution.

Ann was so emotional and so persuasive that evening that eventually I consented to walk across with her to the House of Commons. There I got hold of Desmond Donnelly who was Labour MP for Milford Haven and an old friend. He had already intervened in the chamber that afternoon in an effort to procure a debate by moving a motion to secure the adjournment of the house 'to call attention to a definite matter of urgent public importance, namely, the action of Mr Speaker in directing that the motion submitted by the honourable member for Nelson and Colne should not appear on the Order Paper today'. The Speaker had ruled him out of order because the actions of the Speaker could not be the cause for the adjournment of the House.

Desmond managed to get Maxwell Fyfe to agree to see us, provided it was entirely informal and off-the-record. That may have been quite a generous move on the part of the Home Secretary because Desmond had in the chamber that afternoon been accusing him of having improperly 'got at' the Speaker; or perhaps it was as a result of that accusation and in order that he could convince Desmond that in reality he had had nothing whatsoever to do with the Speaker's decision.

Desmond collected Barbara Castle and the four of us went to see Maxwell Fyfe in his room.

*

He was very emphatic that he had nothing whatsoever to do with the removal of Sydney Silverman's motion from the order paper and had not at any time even discussed the matter with the Speaker. He was cold, chilly and indifferent, sitting at his desk. He listened to all the arguments we could raise about why Bentley should be reprieved. Barbara was particularly eloquent and moving. Then he made us promise not to quote him in public and he gave his reasons for not reprieving Bentley.

First, he said that if he reprieved Bentley he could have the whole of the judiciary, led by Lord Goddard, at his throat.

I asked him directly whether in forwarding the recommendation of the jury Goddard had recommended mercy or not. He told me that far from concurring with the recommendation of the jury Goddard had in writing and personally in conversation pressed him to ensure that the death sentence was carried out.

Secondly, he said that if he reprieved Bentley he would have the whole of the Cabinet at his throat, led by Churchill.

I have no way of knowing whether that was true. However, there was no doubt that the punishment of criminals was at that time a highly party political issue and the Conservatives were anxious to show that they were hard on crime. I don't doubt that there were members of the government who pressurised the Home Secretary to hang Bentley.

Thirdly, he said that if he reprieved Bentley he would have a near insurrection in the police force on his hands.

The Home Secretary confirmed that in his autobiography: 'In the Bentley case I had the additional question of the possible effect of my decision upon the police force by whom the murder of a police officer is justly regarded as the most serious of crimes.'

In that I felt he had a point. Only four years earlier a police officer had been killed by a twenty-two-year-old Army deserter called Donald Thomas. PC Nat Edgar had been shot three times when he was questioning Thomas about an alleged house-breaking. At the time an amendment to the Criminal Justice Bill then before the House of Commons was moved by Sydney Silverman MP. It proposed the abolition of the death penalty for a period of five years. It was opposed by the Labour Government, and all the 'pay-roll' members had voted against it. Nevertheless the amendment was carried by 245 votes to 222. The following day the Home Secretary, Chuter Ede, announced that he would advise the King to commute all death sentences. There was at that time no criticism from the Conservative opposition. It seemed reasonable enough to them that, if the House of Commons had voted to suspend hanging for a trial period of five years, it would be barbaric to go on hanging convicts. However, the decision to reprieve Donald Thomas created a complete uproar in the police, bordering on an insurrection. Little of it surfaced in public, although the *Police Chronicle* guardedly wrote: 'There is little doubt that the decision of the House of Commons is being received with grave apprehension by members of the Police Service.'

Finally, said Maxwell Fyfe, if he did reprieve Bentley, gangs of youths would roam the country with those under 16 armed and willing to kill police officers or others who stood in their way. His widow, Countess de la Warr, later told Fenton Bresler: 'His reasoning was … if a young man of Bentley's age got off because he went out on that kind of enterprise with an even younger man who did not hang, it would happen again. It would be an encouragement to similar exploits in the future.'

Picking up his papers from his desk and beginning to stuff them into a briefcase, he added: 'Everything you have urged in his favour, his feeble-mindedness, his illiteracy, his epilepsy and so on, merely goes to confirm the conclusion that I had already come to. He is a young man that society can well do without.' He then went home and, according to his autobiography: 'After a few lunatic calls, we had the telephone switched off again.' He went to bed and no doubt slept the sleep of one who had done his duty.

Whether Maxwell Fyfe really understood what it was all about is doubtful. In his autobiography he quoted the words Bentley was alleged to have spoken as 'Give it him, Chris'. He also claimed that Craig had lodged an appeal to the Court of Criminal Appeal.

*

The day after the trial the *Daily Mirror* came out with a headline

137

WILL BENTLEY HANG? It referred to a memorandum laid by the Home Office before the Royal Commission on Capital Punishment which said: 'The Home Secretary always attaches weight to a recommendation to mercy from the jury. He would be very reluctant to disregard such a recommendation *if it is concurred with by the judge*' (my italics).

What advice then did Lord Goddard give to the Home Secretary? Certainly he expressed no concurrence with the recommendation of the jury in public, as many another judge might have done.

Later, when he was 93, he said, according to David Yallop: 'I thought Bentley was going to be reprieved. He certainly should have been. There is no doubt whatsoever in my mind, Bentley should have been reprieved.' After his death, the *Times* diarist quoted him as saying that he had been 'very unhappy about Bentley having been hanged'. This prompted the *Times* columnist Bernard Levin to write: 'If Goddard did indeed say that, it was a breathtaking piece of hypocrisy, in view of his conduct of the case.'

It was indeed. For far from passing on the recommendation of the jury with a concurrence, he passed it with a recommendation that it should be ignored and that Bentley should be hanged.

That is entirely consistent with his conduct at the time. Later that same year, he was lavish in his praise of the Home Secretary for having hanged Bentley in the important speech made by the Lord Chief Justice at the Lord Mayor's annual banquet for the judges. He then said:

There are signs, not great signs, that the wave of violent crime is to some extent receding. I think I can say that I attribute that, at any rate to great extent, to the firm attitude of the Home Secretary in refusing to interfere with the due course of justice in a recent case in which great pressure was brought on him at the beginning of the year.

He was still of the same opinion a few years later, when he allowed himself to be interviewed by Fenton Bresler, who was engaged in writing his 'official' biography. Bresler claims to have

138

kept his notes of the interview, which took place in Goddard's flat in Queen Elizabeth Building in the Temple on 12 January 1962:

> Although Craig's offence was the greater of the two, they were equally guilty of murder and should equally have been hanged.
>
> Once Parliament has said that persons can be hanged over the age of eighteen I don't see why the Home Secretary should be expected to observe a higher age limit.
>
> Because they couldn't hang the one doesn't mean to say they shouldn't have hung the other.

I entertain no doubt whatever that Goddard, in forwarding the recommendation of the jury to the Home Secretary and in conversations with him, pressed for Bentley to be hanged.

Lady de la Warr told Fenton Bresler: 'I would have said that David did discuss it with Rayner [Goddard]. I think he always discussed a capital case with the judge.'

Goddard is supposed to have assured his housekeeper, who thought it terribly unfair that Bentley should be hanged whereas Craig could not be, 'Don't worry. He won't be hung.'

But Maxwell Fyfe's widow has the correct explanation of that: 'He could have said it to his housekeeper in a derogatory sense. He would have been frightened that David would have been too weak to stick to his guns.'

*

Was there political pressure from the Cabinet on Maxwell Fyfe not to reprieve Bentley?

It is highly probable that there were others in Cabinet, led by Anthony Eden, who put pressure on the Home Secretary. For the issue of hanging was then a highly party political issue.

In 1947 the Labour Government had put forward to Parliament an Bill designed to reform the criminal law. It proposed the abolition of penal servitude, hard labour and flogging with the cat-o'-nine-tails, an instrument of torture

139

made from whipcord. It was to this Bill that an amendment was proposed by Sydney Silverman which would suspend hanging for a period of five years. The Act came before the House of Lords on 27 April 1948. Lord Goddard took the opportunity to make his maiden speech in the House, and denounced the Silverman amendment.

In June 1948, the Bill came before the Lords on the committee stage. Goddard spoke once again and this time he attacked the Labour Home Secretary, Chuter Ede, for commuting death sentences while the matter was before Parliament. His attack was savage, claiming that the Home Secretary's action was unconstitutional.

'If this is not altering the law by administrative action,' he claimed, 'I do not know what is.' 'If the law of this country is to be respected, it must be in accordance with public conscience.' He asserted that over 80 per cent of the people were in favour of hanging and that *vox populi, vox Dei*, 'the voice of the people is the voice of God'.

The House of Lords rejected the Silverman amendment by 181 to 28.

Lord Goddard's suggestion that the action of Chuter Ede in reprieving all convicted murderers after the House of Commons had voted to abolish the death penalty was a constitutional breach was taken up by Anthony Eden in the House of Commons when the Bill returned there. He gave a long and righteous speech in which he repeatedly referred to this 'grave breach of the constitution'. Herbert Morrison, then Leader of the House of Commons, replied that he found it surprising that the opposition had not raised this point two months earlier when the announcement was made in the House of Commons.

If anything was unconstitutional, it was the Lord Chief Justice publicly criticising the government of the day and actively intervening and drumming up support in the House of Lords to wreck a measure which had been approved by a free vote of the House of Commons. In the end, when the Bill returned to the Commons, Sydney Silverman was persuaded to drop his amendment, since the Lords were determined to wreck the whole Bill if hanging was abolished. It is a strange form of democracy in which a body, wholly unelected, can overrule the decisions of elected members.

The Act, much amended, did eventually pass into law. But Lord Goddard, on and off the Bench, continued his political campaign for the reintroduction of flogging.

'This case and others like it must give one seriously to think whether the modern methods of dealing with young criminals are not to some extent responsible for these outrages' was his comment from the Bench in one case. 'It is not for me to criticise the wisdom of Parliament that prevents me doing what might have been done eighteen months ago.'

It was not for him, he admitted, to criticise the legislature but of course he was doing just that. He did so impliedly and expressly on every possible occasion. In doing so he became a party political activist, abusing his position on the Bench to undermine the government of the day, which had appointed him, and promote the interests of the Conservatives – for which he had once stood as a candidate.

The judiciary in this country, in theory but never in practice, is independent of the executive power. In fact throughout history they have been the servile tools of the executive, whether it be a monarch or a prime minister – 'Lions under the throne', as Coke termed them. Goddard was unlawful and criminal in his abuse of the judicial office for party political purposes.

On 3 July 1952, during the banquet given annually to the judges by the City of London, he took advantage of the occasion to denounce 'the great and disturbing increase of crime which is disgracing this country at the present but more especially the crimes of violence which are as prevalent'. He attributed this directly to the recent Act of Parliament which discontinued flogging and birching and had led thugs to believe that violence was worthwhile. 'The remedy is to restore corporal punishment and to extend, not limit, it.'

In fact, not that he cared to mention it, after the Criminal Justice Act 1948, crimes of violence for which flogging could previously be administered had diminished from 841 cases in 1947 to 633 in 1951.

But it was at that time all good party political propaganda.

There can be little doubt that Goddard's calculated political campaign, supported by the Conservative Women's Central Advisory Committee, the phoney Conservative organised Women's Guild of Empire and the equally phoney Conservative Housewives League was, in part, responsible for returning the Conservatives to power. They were the ones who upheld 'law and order' and the Labour Party were the ones who supported crime and criminals.

So as 1952 ended with Derek Bentley under sentence of death, hanging was not merely a political issue but a *party* political issue.

*

By half-past eight on the morning of 28 January 1953 a crowd of something like a thousand people had gathered outside Wandsworth Prison. There were scuffles between sections of the crowd and police who were guarding the gates.

At nine o'clock the crowd, led by Mrs Van der Elst, sang 'Abide with Me' and the 23rd Psalm, 'The Lord's my Shepherd'. Shortly afterwards a warder came out with two notices to put in a glass case. One recorded the execution of Derek Bentley; the other was a certificate from the Prison Medical Officer that he was dead. There was a scuffle, the glass of the notice case was smashed, and there was fighting between sections of the crowd and the police.

Maxwell Fyfe was at home in his flat in Gray's Inn eating his breakfast with his telephone still disconnected. Two years later he was made Lord Chancellor and ennobled as Lord Kilmuir.

10

Repercussions

In all professions there is a 'jealousy barrier'. Break through it and you are immune from criticism by fellow members of the profession. The other side of it, if you do too well too quickly, you are the subject of hatred.

At the time I was involved in the Craig and Bentley case, I had not broken through the jealousy barrier.

When somebody comes initially to the Bar he is entitled to purchase a blue bag with his initials on it in which to carry his wig box, his gown and collar box. If he is subsequently led by a Queen's Counsel who is pleased with his work, the silk can, at his own expense, give the junior a red bag. Lord Denning had been seven years in practice before he was given a red bag. I was given one in my first year, and it did not please the North Eastern Circuit at all. Still less did it please them that I was widely suspected of making in my first year at the Bar, for six months of which I was in pupillage to Rudolph Lyons, more money than anybody had ever made before in his first year. It was largely luck, because shortly after I joined 38 Park Square the head of chambers, Ralph Cleworth, took silk and much of his practice, together with his junior's gown, fell on my shoulders. Mr Justice Hallett, one of the most detested and feared of all judges, did me a great deal of good in one week at York assizes.

I had gone there with several Poor Prisoners' Defence briefs. The first case which came on for trial before Hallett was one in which two young RAF men were charged with arson. They had been attending a course at an RAF fire-fighting school near York and, coming back from the town drunk one night, they thought it might be funny if there were a fire next door to the fire-fighting school. So they threw lighted matches at a hay stack. Much to their horror it went up in flames.

My defence was that they were too drunk to have the intent necessary to commit the offence of arson. Hallett interrupted me repeatedly in cross-examination, seven times in the course of my address to the jury, and showed himself up as what he was: a nasty bully. The jury, much to my surprise, acquitted them. Upon which Hallett, having ordered their discharge, said in a loud voice to Hugh Radcliffe, the Clerk of the Assize: 'Pathetic these rural juries. Discharge this lot.' So the jurors went home early.

All waiting jurors were seated in the gallery and listening. They concluded that Hallett was a bastard, so I came away with highly improbable acquittals in all my cases. Solicitors crowded the court to see this young man who was 'standing up to Hallett' – something which few counsel cared to do.

*

The North Eastern Circuit went into a mouth-frothing paroxysm of rage after I had appeared in the Craig and Bentley trial.

There were of course honourable exceptions. One was Geoffrey Baker, now a circuit judge; another was Jim Pickles, who was at Leeds University with me, also a circuit judge who has repeatedly had rows with the Lord Chancellor and who recently termed the present Lord Chief Justice 'a dinosaur'. Another was Tony Barber, always a good fellow.

My name had been in all the papers. My speech for the defence of Craig had filled the front and back pages of Britain's then biggest-selling daily newspaper, the *Daily Mirror*. It was an unforgivable crime. The deputy leader of the North Eastern Circuit, Raymond Hinchcliffe QC, sent his clerk, Harrison, to find out from my clerk how I had come to be given the brief. My loyal clerk rebuffed him. Then he was sent to find out from my instructing solicitor, Nelson, why I had been given the brief. All the joy he got there was 'Craig's family told me to brief Parris'.

Frustrated in his efforts to prove that I had myself in some way procured a brief which yielded me an insignificant sum and cost me a great deal of time and money, Hinchcliffe then had me arraigned before the Grand Court of the North Eastern Circuit on charges of improper conduct in procuring publicity for myself by communicating with newspapers. This all seems laughable in 1990 when firms of solicitors engage non-lawyers as 'marketing managers', with the status of a partner, and heads of barristers' chambers, advised by a report prepared for the Bar Council by leading accountants, are into public relations, marketing and self-promotion. But in my day, even a sniff of self-sought publicity by a junior counsel was regarded as disgraceful, not merely as a breach of professional conduct but as an ungentlemanly thing to do. In those days a gentleman kept his name out of the papers, his body out of prison and his soul out of hell – though he was less enthusiastic about the third part of the trilogy.

*

So, after acrimonious correspondence I was once again – it will be recalled that I had been tried once before for allowing a photograph of myself to appear in a Bradford paper a year before I started practising at the Bar – arraigned before the Grand Court of the North Eastern Circuit. I was charged with giving information to the Press about myself in respect of two items.

The first was a piece which appeared in the *Daily Mirror* about how the characters who were due to appear in court next day for the trial of Craig and Bentley had spent their evening. Christmas Humphreys had apparently spent the evening giving a lecture to a Buddhist Society. Frank Cassels had spent his evening listening to a recording of an opera. Neither so far as I ever learnt was required to account to anybody as to how the newspaper acquired that information.

According to the newspaper, I had spent the evening in my London club, the National, going over my brief. I was able to tell the Grand Court that the information was entirely erroneous. But I was inhibited by various considerations from telling them

145

what I had in fact done. The truth was that I had spent a much more pleasant evening than the newspaper reported. I had dinner with a girl-friend and then went to bed with her in her flat before returning about midnight to my room in the Club.

The other charge concerned an item which appeared in the *Daily Express* in the William Hickey column:

There may be no headlines for Edward [sic] Parris this week. There will still be plenty of work. Parris, who made a great impression as Craig's defending counsel at the Old Bailey, is back in Leeds. He has a divorce case today and enough briefs to keep him busy 15 hours a day.

More headlines are in store for Mr Parris. At 37 [sic] he is an up-and-coming man, and has just been asked to take on another murder defence – his eleventh. He has not been out of court for a day since he came back from his holidays at the end of September. These he spent, as usual, in Corsica – in that fascinating new sport, under-water fishing.

The primitive life there attracts him. It is a complete change from the formalism of law courts with their strict etiquette, their robes and wigs. He has bought a piece of land on the island and has hopes of building there and settling down.

Escapism? Why not?

If the members of the circuit had not all been in such a state, they would have realised that if I had myself provided the information on which that paragraph was based I would at least have ensured that my name and age and other details were printed correctly. But I was given a very rough time, before I was eventually exonerated. I was able to assure them categorically that I had not given any of this information to any journalist. That was the truth, the whole truth and nothing but the truth.

Some consolation was afforded me by Mr Justice Donovan, as he then was, who took me on one side at a cocktail party and told me not to be upset by 'this kid's play'. 'Why didn't you tell the silly buggers to go and inquire where the *Express* got the information about Shawcross?' he said. Immediately preceding the Hickey paragraph about me was one which named the exact brief fee and refresher which Sir Hartley Shawcross was to receive for appearing in the Aden Courts on behalf of the Anglo-Iranian Oil Company.

But this judge's attitude was not general. Most of the local Bar were convinced that, although they couldn't prove it, in some mysterious way I could control what was published about me in the *Daily Express*. Perhaps it was to save me from embarrassment of this nature that the counsel who read the proof of Harry Proctor's entertaining book *The Street of Disillusion* advised the deletion of all the flattering references in it to me. But before long, the circuit was given another opportunity to strike at me.

*

The pleasure of attending a Labour Party public meeting on a wet Sunday evening in Bradford in January 1953 will probably have been denied to most who read these words, if only because it was a pleasure shared by very few. Except at election times, or when Nye Bevan paid a visit, the large hall at the Mechanics Institute would be occupied by a handful of faithfuls, many of whom had been in at the foundation of the party.

It was, in fact, not the most exhilarating of meetings; but as I was the prospective candidate for the North Bradford constituency, it was my duty to be present and to speak. On such occasions I tried to find some topic to talk about which would not be covered by any of the usual speakers. On 18 January 1953 I chose 'Crime and Punishment'.

Law and order was a highly political issue. The Conservative Party, quite untruthfully, always portrayed the Labour Party as being soft on crime. They still do. 'Tories turn to crime as potential vote winner' was a headline in the *Glasgow Herald* during the Conservatives' conference in 1990, in spite of the fact that – not surprisingly, in view of her ethics and conduct – Mrs Thatcher's reign resulted in the biggest increase in crime this country has ever seen.

On 18 January 1953 Bentley had not yet been hanged – that was to come on the 28th – but his appeal had been dismissed on the 13th. His fate therefore lay with the Home Secretary. Although I could not directly raise the topic I hoped that, if what I had to say about the death penalty was reported, it might have some influence on his mind.

There was also a more important purpose. Throughout the previous year Lord Goddard had, in the House of Lords and on such inappropriate occasions as the Lord Mayor's annual banquet for the judge, been advocating the return of 'flogging', even though it had been abolished in 1948. Even on the Bench he advocated physical violence to offenders, as when on 3 December 1952, he regretted that somebody could not give 'a thundering good beating' to two boys, one 17 and the other 14, who appeared before him at the Old Bailey. Unfortunately, if he had read the Probation Officer's report before him, he would have found out that they had been regularly beaten by a savage drunken father almost every night.

Michael Foot had some words to say about the observations of Lord Goddard shortly afterwards in the *Daily Herald*:

> When is a judge not a judge?
>
> That novel conundrum is posed by some recent utterances of Lord Goddard, Lord Chief Justice of England. As a judge his duty is to administer the law ...
>
> But Lord Goddard is not only a judge. He also has another profession. He is also a propagandist. He holds strong views on how the law ought to be changed.
>
> That he has every right to do. But sometimes he seems to express the same views in a court of law.
>
> Who then is speaking?
>
> Is it Lord Goddard, the judge, or Lord Goddard, the would-be law maker?
>
> In short, should not Lord Goddard save his opinions on corporal punishment for the House of Lords?

There was a more immediate reason for me to deal with the topic. Four days earlier, on 14 January 1953, a Tory MP Eric

10. Repercussions

Bullins had put down a Private Member's Bill to restore birching. The following evening, Lord Chorley QC, a distinguished constitutional lawyer and a barrister, said at a public meeting in London:

> It is difficult for Englishmen not to feel shame when the Lord Chief Justice is leading a crusade to bring back this form of punishment.
>
> There can be no doubt that the fact that the Lord Chief Justice has been using his position in the way he has is one of the main reasons why this agitation for the restoration of flogging has become so prominent.

He was followed by F.T. Willey MP, a member of the Bar and of my own North Eastern Circuit:

> Who does the Lord Chief Justice think he is?
>
> We have had a full discussion in Parliament, of which Lord Goddard is a member. He failed to persuade Parliament that he was right.
>
> He is now saying Parliament was wrong. This is intolerable. This is very wrong.

*

It was in the midst of this controversy that I made my own speech. Much of it was a plea for the abolition of capital punishment. None of that was reported in the Press. But towards the end I referred to the 'present emotional campaign for the re-introduction of flogging' and said that the unfortunate thing about it was that it was largely – almost entirely – instigated by Lord Goddard. According to Press reports, I said:

> At the moment Lord Goddard is rather like the cat with two heads which figured in a recent law case. One head is the judge's, the other the politician's. I have to stroke the whiskers on one of those heads. The whiskers on the other I am entitled to twist.

149

I proceeded to discuss the constitutional position of a judge, and added that I thought it unfortunate that any judge should engage in a political campaign the real substance of which was criticism of the wisdom of Parliament in passing the Criminal Justice Act:

> The public are entitled to think that anyone who holds high judicial office will be a model of courtesy, fairness and impartiality. For that reason alone it is undesirable that anybody holding high judicial office should place himself in a position where he must be criticised for political utterances.

I then went on to quote parts of various of Lord Goddard's speeches and to criticise them at length.

As to what followed next, there was a considerable difference in the newspaper reports. The *Daily Telegraph* (which one normally assumes is a accurate newspaper) reported me as saying that I could not say anything about the manner in which the Lord Chief Justice conducted criminal trials. The *Manchester Guardian* had another slightly different version which was, in substance, the same. All the reports are substantially agreed that I then continued:

> But I am entitled to say that many of his recent utterances in the House of Lords are sensational and untruthful nonsense. Many of the Members of that House now regard them with complete contempt. Another judicial officer, the Lord Chancellor – who, incidentally, is the only one entitled to engage in politics – is as firmly opposed to the reintroduction of corporal punishment as Lord Goddard is in favour of it. But because the things the Lord Chancellor says are not sensational, are presented with restraint and sanity ... they are not so well known as the ... outbursts of Lord Goddard.

Only the *Yorkshire Post* carried words which suggested that I had criticised the way Lord Goddard conducted criminal trials.

10. Repercussions

Linton Andrews had had his revenge. The words the *Yorkshire Post* reported me as saying, which I certainly did not say, were:

> Unfortunately, I am precluded from expressing in public the universal consensus in the legal profession about the manner in which he conducts criminal trials.

Had I said it, it would of course have been true.

*

In truth I had said no more than what Chorley and Willey, both barristers, had said about Goddard: that I thought it unconstitutional that the Lord Chief Justice should be running a public campaign to bring controversial legislation to be passed by Parliament. No doubt my observations were rather more colourful than theirs, but they said essentially the same thing. Nothing happened to them.

Three months later I was hauled up in front of the Benchers of Gray's Inn for criticising the conduct of Lord Goddard *as a judge*, and the accusation was based on the report in the *Yorkshire Post*. The *Daily Telegraph* was not quoted.

The day on which I was before the Benchers, my master in law, Rudolph Lyons, became a Queen's Counsel. As I remarked at the time, the day Rudolph took silk, I took sack-cloth. I was suspended from practice for four months.

It was, I have always firmly believed, a punishment for what I said that I *was* entitled to say, not for anything I may have said that I was not entitled to say. Moreover the proceedings against me were novel in that, while earlier it might have been regarded as impolitic for a barrister to criticise a judge, there was no recorded case of any barrister having been punished for it. Indeed, fifty years before, Sir Edward Clark KC repeatedly accused Mr Justice Hawkins, both verbally and in writing, of being 'a wicked judge and a wicked man'. The Benchers of his Inn took no action against him. Nobody then suggested that it was unprofessional conduct. It may be, of course, that what is not unprofessional for a Queen's Counsel is unprofessional for

151

small fry. It would only be in keeping with the practice of the rest of our law if the Inns had one rule for the rich and another for the poor.

The cost of my suspension was not inconsiderable. Not only did I lose the briefs for which I had already done the pleadings, but also many cases in which I would otherwise have been instructed to do the pleadings which came on for trial after I had returned. In all, I reckoned it was equivalent to a fine of £4,000, equivalent to ten times that amount in 1991 terms.

Some things about the affair I will, of course, always regret. One was that on the morning of the very day on which I was suspended I received instructions and had a conference in the case of a man charged with murder. The brief was to be very well marked, for a newspaper was providing funds for his defence. The name of the accused was John Henry Christie. His crimes, including that of getting an innocent man hanged for one of them, will not be forgotten in legal history.

Another thing I regret is the way the incident of my suspension has been treated by Lord Denning in his book *The Road to Justice*, which may well come to be regarded by subsequent generations of lawyers as an accurate account of the affair. There he writes:

A few years ago a barrister in a public speech accused the Lord Chief Justice of being harsh towards accused persons. This is what he said: 'The public are entitled to think anyone who holds high judicial office will be a model of courtesy, fairness and impartiality. I cannot express the universal consensus of legal opinion about the manner in which the Lord Chief Justice now conducts trials – I cannot say anything about that.'

In no way did I ever suggest that Lord Goddard was being harsh to accused persons. (Had I done so, of course, it would have been perfectly true.) The interesting thing about my speech was that it was instigated by the Lord Chancellor who was in office when Lord Goddard was appointed Lord Chief Justice. In very frank comments he told me that Goddard was a disgrace to the Bench and that his campaign to reintroduce flogging and preserve capital punishment was 'intolerable and unconstitutional'. He added: 'I can't say anything about it, but why don't you have a go at him?'

*

My suspension did not seem to have a lasting effect on my practice. In fact my receipts the following year were double those of the previous year. I returned after four months sailing the Mediterranean two stones lighter, bronzed and very much fitter. I also attracted a good deal of sympathy. Sir Godfrey Russell-Vick, leader of the Bar, said to me, 'Why didn't you come and see me, John m'boy? I'd have got the whole thing quashed. You should have done what I always did as a Liberal candidate – distribute an innocuous Press Release and then say whatever you liked.'

My opinions also seemed to commend me to a number of judges. Lord Merriman, President of the then Probate, Divorce and Admiralty Division, notorious for being an exceptionally difficult judge, was especially kind to me.

*

Nor did Goddard himself hold it against me. It was not long after the end of my suspension that I was given a returned brief of Ernest Ould to appear before Goddard in London. Our client had bought some allegedly reconditioned army lorries from the defendant, all of which had proved to be broken-down wrecks. Unfortunately Ernest, who usually dictated his pleadings at 8.30 am in the morning into a primitive dictaphone, had, I thought, failed to plead the case properly. He was, as I have recorded earlier, a brilliant and persistent advocate; but he was a poor lawyer and an even worse pleader. As I read the pleadings and the brief on the train to London, I thought the only chance of winning was to ignore the pleadings and open the case on the facts.

So, when I rose to open the case before Lord Goddard, I said:

153

'If your lordship will allow me, I will open the facts before referring to the pleadings.'

In the middle of my opening, Goddard intervened: 'Mr Parris, why shouldn't your client have his money back?'

I realised I had got him on the hook. 'My lord, perhaps my friend can explain that,' and I sat down.

Counsel for the defendant got up and stuttered something. Goddard seemed to pay no attention to what he said and picked his nose, looked at the result and ate it. Although I had not finished my opening, he said: 'Call your evidence, Mr Parris.'

So I put my client into the box. Goddard took a note of what he had to say. Counsel on the other side rose to cross-examine him.

'You want to cross-examine him?' Goddard said, in a tone of total incredulity. 'Very well.' He paid no attention whatsoever to the cross-examination and made no attempt to record any of it. At the end of my client's evidence, he said: 'That's all you want, isn't it, Mr Parris?'

'If your lordship will bear with me, if this case goes any further, I would like to call another witness.'

'Very well, if you please, but many cases are lost because of too much evidence, you know.'

He did not make a note of the evidence of my second witness. He then turned to my opponent: 'You'd better give your client some advice, hadn't you?'

That is exactly what my adversary did; he submitted to judgment. A case scheduled to last two days was over in a little more than 20 minutes.

As I went out of the court into the corridor outside I heard the defendant say to his counsel: 'That bugger had the judge eating out of his hand.'

I shared his sentiments. The defendant hadn't had a fair trial. Goddard, as usual, had made up his mind very early in the trial and nothing could have changed it. In this particular instance I think he was right, but nothing can excuse the fact that it is not the way justice should be done in England.

11

Who Killed PC Miles?

As is abundantly apparent, both Craig and Bentley believed that a bullet from Craig's gun had killed the unfortunate PC Miles; and so did everybody concerned with the case.

However, in 1971 there was published a book by a journalist David Yallop, entitled *To Encourage the Others*. Yallop has since become a millionaire as a result of a later book in which he convincingly argued that Pope John was murdered by his entourage when he was given an overdose of a drug taken for a heart condition, because he had showed himself intent on investigating the connection between the Mafia and the Vatican Bank. Yallop interviewed almost everybody connected with this case from Lord Goddard to Christopher Craig, including Frank Cassels. He did not, however, interview me, although I am quoted in a preface entitled 'An Open Letter to the Home Secretary' as telling him:

> I have always considered that everybody connected with the case – from Lord Goddard to the most humble court attendant – entertained no doubt but that Bentley was entirely innocent of the crime with which he was charged. But many of them, including Lord Goddard, believed that it was in the public interest that somebody, anybody, should die because a police officer had been killed.
>
> In short, Bentley was a vicarious sacrifice, the innocent scapegoat released into the desert to die and thus to bear away into oblivion the guilt of a whole people.

It ought perhaps to have been made plain that Yallop did not see me until his book was already in proof. Otherwise I might have been able to contribute some evidence which supported his conclusions.

Furthermore, he has inaccurately summarised what I said. I told him, as I have said in my book *Most of My Murders*, and as I now say, that there was evidence from which a jury could properly have convicted Bentley of engaging in a joint venture to commit violence to resist arrest, which did not necessarily come to an end with his arrest, but that I thought it unlikely that a jury would have convicted – as indeed did the prosecution, because they invented the words 'Let him have it, Chris'. It was upon these that Bentley was convicted, and without them he would not, in my view, have been convicted.

But that probably was all too subtle for a journalist. At no time did I say that I, or anybody else, thought that Bentley was 'entirely innocent'. What I did say was that, unless the prosecution had satisfied the jury that in fact he did utter the words 'Let him have it, Chris' and that that was an incitement to shoot at a police officer, he would not have been convicted.

*

The crux of David Yallop's book was that, although Christopher Craig thought then, and still thinks, that it was a shot from his gun which killed PC Miles, it was in fact a shot from a police weapon fired from somewhere in the region of No. 26 Tamworth Road or from the roof of the warehouse in its vicinity. In that he relied upon what I had elicited in cross-examination of the forensic expert, Lewis Nickolls:

> Turning to the revolver, one of the effects of sawing off the barrel is, of course, to remove the sight.
> You do.
> The second thing is this, that when the rifling is removed the weapon becomes wholly inaccurate.
> It becomes less accurate.
> Well, how inaccurate would you say that would make it?

11. Who Killed PC Miles?

I should say that this weapon, certainly in the hands of a person unaccustomed to firing it, was quite an inaccurate weapon.

Then you would agree with me that it would be wholly inaccurate?

Not quite – no sir, I think a person could train himself to use it.

May I put it to you that it would be inaccurate to the degree of six feet at a range of thirty-nine feet?

Oh, yes.

Quite as much as that?

I think it would be of that order, yes.

Lewis Nickolls, who had formerly been at the Harrogate Forensic Laboratory, in which connection I had come across him previously, was as anxious as all so-called forensic experts from the Home Office to help the prosecution. His reply that a person could train himself to use a wildly inaccurate weapon was, of course, nonsense. To start with, even a trained expert holding an intact weapon in both hands could not be certain of hitting anybody across a room with a .45 calibre or the similar revolver the .455 Eley. They have a most vicious kick.

All this I learned, as I have noted, from the ballistics expert, Major Chivers. Nickolls happily confirmed what he had advised me about the effectiveness of a sawn-off revolver, so I did not have to call him. With an inaccuracy of 6 feet at 39-feet range – the distance at which Miles, it was claimed, had been shot, that meant 6 feet either side of the target: that is 12 feet in all. My comment to the jury was therefore perfectly justified:

How did PC Miles come to receive a bullet right through his forehead? You have heard what has been said about this revolver and the ammunition, and you may conclude that it was a tragic, unfortunate, million-to-one shot, because Mr Nickolls told you that at that range of 39 feet the weapon would be inaccurate by at least 6 feet. It may be – and the defence do not purpose to explain it – that that bullet struck the parapet and ricochetted off; it may be that although

157

aimed at No. 30, the deviation of the bullet was much greater than 6 feet; it may be that the whole thing swerved right round in the boy's hand. Members of the jury, is not everything you know about the weapon and everything you know about the events of that night consistent with Craig's story that it was an unhappy, miserable, tragic accident that PC Miles was even injured? I say that the events of that night, looked at dispassionately and impartially, corroborate what Christopher Craig has told you. He says: 'I never intended any harm at all to those officers. I was banging away to frighten them.'

Yallop's conclusion was as follows:

The fact is that there was not at that time, either before, during, or after the trial, any ballistic evidence to prove that Craig had fired the shot that killed PC Miles. In fact, there was a startling amount of ballistic evidence to prove his innocence.

*

Yallop's contention was that 'PC Miles was the victim of a tragic accident: the bullet which killed him was not from Craig's gun.'
He based this conclusion in part on the pathologist's report on the dead policeman, given by Dr David Haler:

There were two wounds in his head.
One was on the inner side of the left eyebrow and was a typical wound of entry of a large calibre bullet.
The other slightly to the right at the back of the head, was the exit wound of the same bullet.
Death would have been virtually instantaneous.

Yallop points out that neither Frank Cassels nor I cross-examined Haler. For good reason, of course. Our clients had instructed us that PC Miles had been killed by a bullet from Craig's gun.

But a later writer about the case, M.J. Trow, commented:

There were times, certainly, when both Parris and Cassels missed opportunities to challenge witnesses, most obviously perhaps when they failed to cross-examine Dr David Haler, the pathologist, on the nature of the wound which killed Miles.

There was no reason why either of us should have challenged Haler. My client admitted that it was a bullet from his gun, a .45 automatic bullet fired from a .455 revolver, that killed the officer. So did Bentley. As counsel, we could only accept instructions from our clients.

*

However, when Dr Haler was interviewed by Yallop he was asked if he could define a 'large calibre bullet' more precisely. Yallop reported:

He had privately formed the opinion that the wound could have been caused by a bullet of a calibre between .32 and .38.

What Yallop wrote about what Haler had told him was subsequently the subject of a libel action against him and against the *Guardian* newspaper, on the ground that there was an innuendo suggesting that Haler had deliberately suppressed this evidence. Both actions were settled in favour of Haler.

However, Dr Haler has apparently not at any time contested that, in his view, PC Miles had been shot by a bullet of a calibre between .32 and .38.

Various scientific papers have been published on the subject of wounds caused by rifle and revolver bullets, and it is a notoriously difficult question to determine. But if this view was in fact expressed to Yallop and is correct, it means that PC Miles could not have been killed by a bullet from Craig's gun. A .32 to .35 bullet cannot be fired from a .455 weapon. There is no dispute about that. This may be borne out by Yallop's interview with Craig. He writes:

> Craig told me that any shots he had fired in the direction of the roof entrance had been directed well away from the door and were aimed over the garden of No. 30.
> The reason was that he knew that behind the door, as well as two policemen, was his friend Derek Bentley.
> Describing the moment when Miles had jumped out on to the roof, Craig said:
> What I've never been able to understand is how I shot him between the eyes when he was facing away from me and was going the other way.

There is striking confirmation of this point in the interview given to Trow by PC Claude Pain, who was undoubtedly there that night and who claims to have been one of the only two police officers on the roof at the time when Miles was shot. He was, he claims, lying behind the rooflights near the stairhouse door through which Miles emerged:

'The bullet was supposed to have gone into his forehead. How do you get that? If he turns that way to his right, the bullet if it was fired by Craig … should have entered the back of his head.'

Later, he referred to it again: 'Craig's there. If he fired there and if Miles turned right, how did he get that mess in front of his head?'

His evidence also bore out that Craig was shooting over the garden of No. 30, and not towards the stairhead.

*

Had David Yallop consulted me before he wrote his book I might have been able to supply some information to support his thesis, which in essence was that PC Miles was shot by a police officer who was firing a weapon with .32 bullets from the region of No. 30 Tamworth Road.

The day before the trial I went up to have a look at the roof of Barlow & Parker's warehouse. Frank Cassels, I know, did not.

11. Who Killed PC Miles?

I was looking particularly for some mark on the roof to confirm that what Craig had told me was true: particularly that, when a bullet from his gun had hit Fairfax, it was a ricochet from the ground, but also to see whether there were any signs that, when Craig was alleged to have fired at PC Harrison near the chimney stacks, there were any bullet marks which might prove how inaccurate his weapon was.

I discovered nothing that would support Craig's account, apart from a bullet mark on the glass well removed from where PC Harrison was, to which I made reference in the course of the trial. But I did notice two things. When PC Miles came up through the stairhead door he might have been facing left as he turned right. So that the evidence found by Yallop, and confirmed by PC Claude Pain, is ambiguous.

But what is undeniable is this: the door through which PC Miles thrust his way on to the roof, which opened right, had a glass panel at the top. This panel, whether he turned left or right, and whether he was looking left or right, would inevitably have been drilled or shattered by a bullet fired from Craig's gun on the left. No damage was done to that glass window, immediately behind the head of PC Miles, as is evident from photographs taken shortly afterwards which appeared as part of Exhibit No. 1.

At the time I thought it curious, but irrelevant, since my client admitted shooting the officer. If in fact PC Miles was killed by a bullet coming from the bottom right, that is of course an explanation.

I also noticed that there was, on the right hand side of the door frame, a naked piece of wood which could easily have been where a bullet had been lodged and been excavated by a pen knife. That is just the place where a bullet coming from his right might lodge.

At the time, it seemed to have no significance whatever. The police professed not to have found the bullet which killed PC Miles. PC Claude Pain, who claimed to be within eight or nine feet of PC Miles when he was shot, appears doubtful. He was asked by his son, in the course of a recorded interview: 'Why didn't they find the bullet?'

His reply was: 'Well, some people think, perhaps, there might have been an officer round here somewhere ....'

It suggests that the bullet that killed PC Miles in fact was found by the police embedded in the wooden frame to the right of the door entrance. But it was never produced in court because it was a .32 bullet, which could not be fired from Craig's gun and was found in a position where it could not possibly have come from Craig's gun.

*

In opening his case to the jury Christmas Humphreys said: 'The whole of the gun fight seems to have taken place from 20 to 25 minutes.' There was no evidence to support this, but neither of the two counsel for the defence was in a position to dispute it.

However, David Yallop has subjected this scenario to scrutiny.

Mrs Edith Ware had seen two youths climbing over the gate at 9.15 pm. The police were there, according to her evidence at the trial, in about 'four minutes'. This is confirmed by the evidence of PC Claude Pain, only recently available, who was in a police van with DC Fairfax, driven by PC Beecher-Brigden, according to Pain 'a fat bloke who could hardly drive a van'. PC Pain's estimate was 'four minutes tops for journey'. It follows that the police were there no later than 9.20 pm.

Yallop's conclusion was that Craig did not dive from the roof until 10.15 pm at least: therefore double the time postulated by Humphreys – and it may have been much later.

The conclusion therefore is that the prosecution deliberately attenuated the time in which the whole incident took place. Why?

One feasible answer is, in order to disguise the fact that two officers from Scotland Yard, armed with *rifles* firing .32 bullets, had arrived and stationed themselves on the roof of No. 26 Tamworth Road; and that it was they who, shooting in the dark at a moving object, killed PC Miles. Photographers from the Press Association in Central London were there in time to take a picture of Derek Bentley being taken away in a police car between two officers. If they were there then, there was time for officers armed with rifles to have come from Scotland Yard.

11. Who Killed PC Miles?

*

There was positive evidence which established how many shots were in fact fired from Craig's revolver. Three cartridges were found on the roof top. Six were found in the revolver, three of which, although struck by the firing pin, had not exploded. So it seems certain that Craig had fired successfully only six shots.

It is therefore relevant to go through the evidence about the shots that took place. Lord Goddard, in his summing up, said:

> Let me help you to come to a conclusion whether this man was deliberately firing at the officers. The very first shot that he fired hit a police officer, fortunately doing him very little harm. The second shot that was fired, according to Sergeant Fairfax's evidence, was when Bentley was on the ground, because you will remember that what the police officer said was that the first shot caused him to spin round and fall to the ground, and he brought Bentley to the ground. Sergeant Fairfax got up, and while Bentley was on the ground he was trying to pull Bentley up, or get him as a shield, when the prisoner fired a second time. Then other police offers were heard, because the prisoner himself told you he heard police officers coming up the stairs, and then the third shot was fired in the direction of the stairs, and PC Miles fell dead.

After Lord Goddard had concluded his direction to the jury I had to rise to correct him (see p. 118 above):

> Your lordship said that Sergeant Fairfax said it was the third shot which was the fatal one. That would appear to be so from his deposition, but he said in evidence that it was the seventh or eighth. That appears in the cross-examination, my lord.
>
> It may be. This is my note: 'As he fell there was a second shot, and I pulled Bentley before me as a shield.' Then he said he felt Bentley and found the knuckleduster: 'Then Bentley said, "He'll shoot you." Craig had followed us to about 20 feet or something, and then retired to the top

corner. I heard McDonald coming up. I shouted to Craig, "Drop your gun." McDonald said, "What sort of a gun has he got?" Before I could reply, Bentley said, "He's got a .45." '

It is in the cross-examination, my lord. May I give your lordship the note taken by my learned friend: 'The shot that hit PC Miles was not the third shot.'

I have have not got that, but be it so. It may not have been the third. It may have been the fourth, it may have been the fifth, it may have been the sixth. I do not know that it very much matters. It, at any rate, was a shot that he fired after he heard those police officers coming up the staircase. The shot, therefore, which killed PC Miles must have been fired in the direction of the staircase. It does not really seem to me to matter very much whether it was the third shot, or the fifth shot, or the sixth shot.

Of course, it did matter which shot it was that had killed PC Miles, but Lord Goddard had used the fact that it was the third shot to rebut the evidence that Craig was not deliberately firing at police officers. Having made a deadly point against the defence, on a totally inaccurate version of the evidence, he did not retract it but simply swept it aside as a matter of no importance – although he had told the jury earlier that it was a matter of great importance.

*

The evidence of Fairfax under cross-examination by me was in fact as follows:

Now let me see if I understand your story correctly. You say it was the third shot that was fired that was the fatal shot; is that right?

The shot that hit PC Miles, sir? Oh no; to my recollection there were several other shots; but I don't know what he was firing at.

You have not mentioned that hitherto, have you?

No.

You said there was one shot which struck you first of all, then another shot, and the third shot you mentioned was the shot which hit PC Miles?

That is the shot which hit PC Miles; but it certainly was not the third shot.

What other shots were there?

I should say there were somewhere like six or seven shots.

Before the fatal shot?

Before the fatal shot, yes.

Do I understand you correctly; were there six or seven other shots in addition to the ones you told my lord and the jury about?

Yes, that is so.

You had said not a word about those shots until a few moments ago, had you, officer?

No.

Did you see where they came from?

No.

Where were you when they were fired?

I was then round about the doorway marked 'B' and the bottom left hand rooflight.

Later in cross-examination I came back to the point:

So if I am right in my addition, is this your story, two shots to start with, six or seven after that, the fatal one, and one later?

Yes.

That makes either ten or eleven shots in all that you say you heard?

Round about ten shots.

It was about that?

About ten shots, yes.

From that evidence it is clear that the fatal shot was the seventh one heard, and that there were three or four shots after that. Craig's revolver fired no more than six shots. The others must have come from some other weapons.

David Yallop's theory was that they came from hand-guns issued to the detective force of Croydon Police Station. He did not have the advantage that I had of being told long after the event by a police officer who was in the station at the time that two Scotland Yard marksmen with rifles had been sent for and had stationed themselves on the roof of No. 26 Tamworth Road.

That is surmise and speculation. The probability is: that the incident lasted much longer than Christmas Humphreys had alleged; that, in that time, some police officers with weapons firing .32 ammunition arrived on the site; that the fatal bullet, the seventh heard, could not have come from Christopher Craig's gun since only six bullets were in fact fired from it; that if PC Miles had been shot from his left by Craig the top window behind him would inevitably have been penetrated or shattered; that, although PC Miles may perhaps have been looking left as he turned right through the door, the probability is that he was not doing so, and the probability therefore is that he was shot from his right; that the bullet which in fact killed PC Miles was found by the police lodged in the right-hand side of the staircase, but it was found to be a .32 bullet which could not possibly have been fired from Craig's gun.

There was evidence that the sixth shot from Craig's revolver was fired from it *after* PC Miles had been killed. It is contained in the testimony of PC S.L. Stewart who went, according to his evidence, to Barlow & Parker's warehouse at about 9.45 pm. He claimed to have heard the sound of shots and then to have climbed up a drainpipe on to the flat roof and there seen the body of PC Miles. He got there, he said, after that officer had been shot:

Could you from there see anybody on the roof?
Yes, I could see Craig.
What was he doing?
He was sitting on the iron railing that ran round the side of the flat roof – sitting on it with his feet out towards the end – and he was holding a revolver in two hands and pointing it towards the stairway on the roof behind which I knew there were some police officers.

166

Look at Exhibit No. 1, the book of photographs. Does the fifth photograph in that book show the place where you saw Craig?

Yes.

On the corner of the roof there?

Yes.

Did you hear him say anything?

Yes. He said, 'Yes, it's a Colt .45. Are you hiding behind a shield? Is it bullet-proof ? Are we going to have a shooting match? It's just what I like. Have they hurt you, Derek?'

Was that all one sentence, or was it a number of disjointed observations?

A number of disjointed sayings he said which I heard from the moment I got into the garden till I was underneath him.

Did you see him do anything?

Yes. He pressed the trigger of the revolver four times and I heard four separate and distinct clicks.

Then what did he do?

He then raised the revolver, pointed it in the air and *I heard the sound of a shot.*

Did he say anything?

He said 'See, it's empty.'

167

12

How Many Youths Were Involved?

In *Most of My Murders*, I suggested that another youth might have been on the rooftop that night besides Craig and Bentley. The theory was not based on instructions from my client, but on inferences drawn from various sources.

The evening after the event there appeared in the stop press column of the *Star*, a London evening paper:

> Police are looking for a third youth believed to have been on the roof of Messrs Barlow & Parker's premises when PC Miles was shot.

Journalists do not print information like that unless they are tipped off by the Metropolitan Police Press Office or some individual officer. This was confirmed by the fact that at one o'clock that morning police went to the house of Norman Parsley, the Dulwich College boy who had invited Derek Bentley to come out that night. I have no information about what they had to say to him, but their arrival there at that hour suggests that they thought he had some knowledge or that he had somehow been involved in the murder of PC Miles. Their pressure on him, however, did induce him to state, after he had described how he met Christopher Craig in the afternoon:

> He said something about 'I have got something on tonight. There is no risk.'
> I rather gathered he meant it was some sort of crookedness. I had nothing to do and was fed up, browned off, and I agreed to go with him.

I did not have a lot of money but thought I might make some.

We went on a bus to South Croydon and on the ride Craig said to me: 'It is easy. All we have to do is to walk up to the door, knock, and then we are in.' He gave me a black gun with a shiny barrel. I was wearing my dad's trilby and had a white scarf over my face; we both had guns.

He described the hold-up and added:

I had the hammer of my gun on an empty chamber, but there were some bullets in the revolving chamber.

After we had left the house, Craig gave me half the money, more than £2 in silver. We went to the pictures in Streatham and then went home ...

We agreed not to use the guns unless we had to.

There was no other evidence to connect him with the crime. It is just as well that this statement was not before the jury in the case of Craig and Bentley, for in its last sentence it was plain that both Craig and Parsley were prepared to use their weapons to avoid arrest.

While the jury were out on the Craig and Bentley case, Lord Goddard dealt with Norman Parsley. Parsley's mitigation was that he had come under the influence of Christopher Craig's 'magnetic personality'. But Goddard said:

It is true you are only sixteen and it is true that you were in company with a young lad who is apparently a serious criminal. But I say at once that if you had been over twenty-one I would have sent you to prison for twelve years.

You covered your face with a mask, took a revolver, and with another armed lad you went to a house and terrified an old lady who might have had a heart attack and died on the spot, and then terrified her old husband for the sake of getting what you could.

You have not once expressed regret for what you have done.

170

12. How Many Youths Were Involved?

I, and other judges, will do our best to let young men know what will happen to them if they do this sort of thing.

He then sentenced Parsley to four years in prison.

There was other evidence, however, which suggested that there was a third youth on the rooftop that night. Mrs Edith Ware gave evidence at the trial that she had seen two men opposite her house, outside Barlow & Parker. She was asked by Mr Bass for the prosecution:

What did you see either or both of them do?

Well, they were just standing there talking for a few minutes and pulling their hats over their eyes. Every time a bus came along they pulled their hats down and stood talking, and then all of a sudden the shorter one of the two jumped right over the fence at the side on the left.

Is there a gate of some kind there?

A black iron gate.

Was it there do you mean?

Yes.

The shorter one got over that gate?

Yes.

What about the second man?

He waited for a few more minutes, and then a motor came round the corner and he waited for that to go by, and when there was no one in sight he jumped over.

Did you lose sight of them after they had gone over the gate?

Yes, completely.

Did you then send for the police?

Yes.

The interesting thing about this is that both men had trilby hats on, which they tipped over their eyes when buses came past. One thing is absolutely certain: if Derek Bentley was one of the two men he was not wearing a trilby. His greased, Marcel-waved hair was his great delight, and the only trilby he ever possessed stayed immaculate in his room at home, long

171

after the event and after he had been hanged. This suggests that Bentley was first over the gate and up on to the roof, and that the two men Mrs Ware saw were Christopher Craig and another person wearing a trilby hat.

My interest in the matter was aroused when, seconds before the door opened to allow Lord Goddard to take his seat on the bench, Christmas Humphreys slid across to me on the comfortable seats in the new court at the Old Bailey and asked: 'I take it you are not going to raise the issue that there may have been a third boy on the roof that night.'

'I have no instructions about that.'

'In which case, we won't raise it.'

It suggested to me that the prosecution knew perfectly well that there was a third youth on the roof that night but chose to suppress the knowledge lest it should be suggested that it was he, rather than Bentley, who uttered the words 'Let him have it, Chris', and that the defendants had likewise suppressed the information because they did not want their mate to be involved in a murder charge.

I did not know then, and I do not know now, what the real truth is about the events on the roof of Barlow & Parker's warehouse that night. But I had whispers from clients in prison that somebody there was boasting that he had been on the roof the night PC Miles was killed.

13

Another Version of Events

In 1988 the wife of a schoolmaster was taking driving lessons in the Isle of Wight. Her instructor, a former police cadet named Raymond Pain, learned from her that her husband was a writer who had had a few novels published. He suggested that his father had information about which a book should be written.

It turned out that his father was Claude Pain, who was one of the police officers who had gone to the roof of Barlow & Parker's warehouse the night PC Miles was killed. The schoolmaster, M.J. Trow, interviewed Claude Pain on tape on Sunday, 4 September 1988 and subsequently, in 1990, published a book, *Let him have it, Chris*, based on that interview.

The recollection of Claude Pain differs radically from the evidence of Fairfax, Harrison and McDonald given at the trial. According to him, that night he had gone to a photography class and was early for his night duty in the station before ten o'clock. Shortly before, the Station Officer, a Sergeant Danny Watson, told him that intruders had been seen on a roof in Tamworth Road. Pain travelled to the scene in a van driven by a PC Beecher-Brigden. As it was leaving the back gates of Croydon Police Station, they came across Detective Fairfax going home from duty.

'What have you got?' he asked.

'Suspects on roof.'

'Right, I'll hop in.'

It took them about four minutes to get to Tamworth Road. Fairfax got out and disappeared. By that time there was a number of people around, and one of them said to Pain, 'I've got some sort of an old ladder. It's up to you. If you want to go up there you can.'

That account differs fundamentally from the evidence given in court. According to that, the officers who had first gone to Tamworth Road in the van were Fairfax and Norman Harrison. Their story was that Fairfax had climbed over the gate and up a vent pipe, while Harrison went round to the back to another road behind the warehouse. Attention has already been drawn to the time discrepancies between the evidence of Fairfax and Harrison.

Pain said: 'Fairfax in his evidence said that he picked up Harrison and we went in the van. He didn't. I never picked that Harrison up at all. He went there on his bike.'

Shortly after their arrival a police car arrived in Tamworth Road. It was driven by PC Miles, with PC McDonald as his wireless operator.

Pain rejects entirely McDonald's evidence that he, McDonald, managed to climb up to the roof. He confirms my impression of that officer at the trial. McDonald said he climbed up the vent pipe. He gave evidence that he had climbed over the gate and up on to the roof but, according to Pain, he never did, as he was a nervous sort of chap. 'Drainpipe! Climb up it? It's ridiculous! He couldn't even ride a bike.' According to Pain, at all material times McDonald was round in Drayton Place and in no position to hear anything. This adds significance to the last sentence in Bentley's allegedly voluntary statement to the police: 'I should have mentioned that after the plain clothes policeman got up the drainpipe and arrested me, another policeman in uniform foll-owed and I heard somebody call him "Mac". He was with us when the other policeman was killed.'

This is, I believe, a comment which was added later when it was decided to enrol McDonald in the cast as one who had heard the fatal words.

*

McDonald swore that Fairfax and he were the only two police officers on the roof before PC Miles was killed. According to Claude Pain, this was untrue; not only was McDonald never there, he himself was.

13. Another Version of Events

Pain climbed up the ladder from *the front* of the building in Tamworth Road. He was on the roof when shooting started and he crawled along and sheltered on the ground behind one of the four rooflights. He believes he was the first one on the roof. His reason was that there was a lot of shouting going on: 'Keep your heads down, there's shooting, there's shooting.' So he lay on the roof top. From there he heard, 'You bastards, you bastards.' He assumed that this had come from Craig. But he categorically denied that Bentley ever said 'Let him have it, Chris' – and he knew and had spoken to Bentley before that night. 'I did not hear it, *because it was not said.*' Pain was still lying behind the rooflights, he claims, when PC Miles opened the door and turned to the right. He was within a few feet of him when he was shot.

'He was a very excitable chap,' Pain told Trow. Miles pushed the door open and made a quick turn. 'I heard the shooting and I saw him go like this – holding his hands to his head – and down he went on his forehead. I crawled along.'

At that stage, Pain did not know who it was, except that it was a uniformed officer.

'I used to play darts with old Sid Miles, and three darts were sticking out of his pocket as he dropped. That's when I felt it had got to be Sid Miles. I sort of moved him, and his face was like a pig, where he must have been running up those stairs, and his heart was beating and then "bang". He got it, didn't he? There was a lot of people came up behind.'

*

Later Claude Pain wrote his notes of the incident in his pocket-book in long hand. He transferred that to an official statement form. He was called to attend the Croydon Magistrates' Court the next day; but he was not called to give evidence then, during the committal proceedings or at the trial. Later he had a discussion with PC Beecher-Brigden in which that officer commented: 'As far as I know, I didn't go there. I didn't pick you up. I didn't exist. It seemed to be all set-up.'

Pain was asked by Trow why he had not revealed all this when he realised that Bentley was going to hang.

175

He said: 'I thought: What's going to happen to me? I had a wife and three kids. Am I going to cause an awful stink? Now what's going to happen to me if I do that. I've got a family. I'm retiring in two years' time. What's going to happen to me? I could be run over by a police car or something like that. You never know because there are so many big voices involved, isn't there?'

*

Thames Television decided to make a programme in effect based upon Trow's book, but they advertised for, and found and interviewed other witnesses to the events on the roof. The programme was produced and directed by Roger Corke, who has a degree in law, and the interviewer was Carole Priest.

They found five eye-witnesses of the events on the roof of Barlow & Parker, none of whom had been called to give evidence at the trial. The testimony of these casts serious doubt upon the evidence given on behalf of the prosecution at the Old Bailey.

Claude Pain himself was interviewed. He was adamant that PC McDonald had never been at any time in the alleyway beside the warehouse, and that he certainly had not climbed up a vent pipe on to the roof. This is what I had suspected at the time. McDonald was too fat and flabby even to have got over the 6-foot gate with spikes which barred entrance to the alleyway, let alone climb up a shaky vent pipe. Pain was equally certain that Fairfax and his captive Derek Bentley were at no time taking cover behind the stairhead. He himself was, he claimed, lying on the floor behind the glass roof. Nobody was behind that stairhead when PC Miles was shot.

In that respect his evidence was confirmed by that of an eye-witness discovered by Thames Television. John Tennant, who lived at No. 31 Tamworth Road, witnessed from his garden the whole of the action on the roof of the warehouse. At no time, he said, had Fairfax or his captive, Derek Bentley, ever been behind the staircase. According to him, the arrest of Bentley had taken place to the right of the lift shaft and at no time before the shooting of PC Miles had there been anybody hiding behind the stairhead.

13. *Another Version of Events*

On television Claude Pain was rather less emphatic that he had been in his interview with Trow. 'At the time when the first shots were fired I was in the alleyway. There was nobody else there, I am absolutely certain. Certainly, I never saw PC McDonald there. It is possible that the words "Let him have it, Chris" were said, but I did not hear them.'

Pain described how he had gone up the ladder and lain down behind the glass roof. There was nobody, he claimed, behind the stairhead; so that when the fatal shot was fired he, lying on the ground, was within inches of the body. According to him, he put out his hand, came into contract with three darts in the pocket of the dead man and realised that it must have been his friend, Sidney Miles. He was adamant that after the murder, the body of Miles was taken down the staircase *before* Bentley was taken down. The evidence of Fairfax and McDonald was to the contrary.

Thames Television interviewed two lay people who were there in the warehouse that night. Douglas Barlow is the son of the warehouse owner, and it was he who had provided the police with the keys to enter it. He was absolutely certain that the body of Miles was taken down the stairs before Bentley was 'frog marched' down the stairs looking 'shocked and white, but not saying anything'.

With him was another employee of Barlow & Parker, Dennis Widcock. His evidence confirmed that of Pain and Barlow: 'The body of PC Miles was brought down the stairs *before* Derek Bentley, held by two police officers, was frog marched down the stairs. Before that happened the lights were put on, illuminating the inside and outside of the warehouse.'

All four new witnesses, Pain, Tennant, Barlow and Widcock, unite in one thing: the evidence that DC Fairfax gave about going back up the staircase armed with a revolver and having a confrontation with Craig was not correct: 'No officer was handed a gun. Nobody else fired a gun after the death of PC Miles.'

*

This, of course, is not in accordance with the evidence given by DC

177

Fairfax at the Old Bailey trial. Examined in chief by Christmas Humphreys:

What happened then?

An officer then jumped from the doorway.

Who was it?

PC Miles; and as he did so, there was a loud report and he fell to the ground. I went out to try and pull him behind cover, and as I did so there was a second loud report. I dropped to one knee and got hold of PC Miles by his shoulders and PC McDonald came forward and got hold of his legs and we pulled him behind the shelter with us. That is the shelter marked 'B'.

Did you examine him and find he had been shot between the eyes and was dead?

Yes.

Then did PC Harrison come up the stairs and take the offensive, so to speak?

Yes; PC Harrison arrived and jumped out of the doorway and rushed round to where I was.

Did you decide to take Bentley downstairs?

Yes.

And did you push him round the door to the entrance of the staircase?

Yes, and pulled him into the entrance there.

What did he say while you were doing that?

As he was pulled into the entrance of the doorway he shouted, 'They're taking me down, Chris.'

Did you hear what was the result of that from Craig?

No.

You went down with Bentley?

Yes.

Were you given something at the bottom of the stairs?

Yes, I was given a pistol.

Did you hand over Bentley to some other officer and return to the roof?

Yes.

178

You mean you were given a pistol by one of the police officers, a police pistol?

Yes.

What happened when you got back to the roof?

I shouted to Craig, 'Drop your gun; I also have a gun', and he shouted back, 'Come on then, copper, let's have it out.' I jumped out of the doorway on to the flat roof, and as I did so there was another flash and a loud report, and I rushed at Craig in a semicircular direction and I fired two shots as I went. Before I reached Craig he vanished over the roof.

What was the gun you were firing?

A .32 automatic pistol.

For the television programme Harrison declined to be interviewed. Fairfax, too, then said that he stood by his evidence in court, but he refused to appear or to answer further questions.

Thames Television sent the video to the Home Secretary, David Waddington, with an invitation to institute a judicial inquiry into the whole case, on the grounds that fresh evidence was now available. The statement of Claude Pain made at the time was available to the prosecution. But none of those made by him or any other officer was made available to the defence: still less those taken from civilian witnesses.

Among those interviewed by Thames Television was a police cadet in the Croydon Police Station the night PC Miles was killed. 'There was a mood of intense anger which I have never experienced before or since.'

Anger enough to induce Detective Inspector Smith to write a script which would result in an epileptic moron being hanged for the death of the officer?

14

A Live Issue

In the famous interview he gave to A.N. Wilson of the *Spectator* in 1990, Lord Denning said that 'The Guildford Four were probably guilty.' He added 'We shouldn't have all these campaigns to get the Birmingham Six released if they'd been hanged. They'd have been forgotten, and the whole community would be satisfied.'

Derek Bentley was hanged. But his case will not go away. He has not been forgotten. The community is not satisfied.

In 1990 three books about the case were published and they were followed by the Thames Television programme to which I have referred. But what Denning now says, as he admits, is what he has always believed. In that he is typical of most judges. They are quite happy to have the innocent hanged. For at heart they are all fascists. They believe in order over justice. The true purpose of the archaic British judicial system is to keep the subjects of the Crown cowed and in their place, by terror if necessary. As A.P. Herbert tried to point out long ago, the real purpose of the legal system from Magna Carta onwards is to keep society smoothly running in the interests of the rich and powerful for their own convenience and comfort. Lord Denning has always thought that maintenance of respect for the legal system was more important than doing justice. To adapt his own motto: *Fiat Lex, ruat Justitia*.

*

In the *Times* in 1990 Bernard Levin wrote:

I remember the Craig-Bentley case for a number of reasons, but one is dominant; I do not exaggerate when I say that it significantly helped to shape my life and work. At the time of the events, which was late 1952, I was just starting my career as a journalist, but so little footing did I have that I was not at all certain that I had found my *métier*, or even, if I had, whether I wanted to pursue it.

The seed which the case planted for me might have borne fruit in one of many professions, and of course there is no need to make such a connection at all; many people, following the case, must have had an identical reaction, without any continuing effect. But from that day forth, I have never allowed myself to believe in the myth – perpetuated in and by our legal process – of the unstained, unstainable Olympian judge, raised high above the courtroom to seek justice and promulgate it. In the Craig-Bentley case, so shameless was the bias of the judge (Lord Chief Justice Goddard), not only in his summing up but in his entire handling of the proceedings, that my image of the Bench was transformed.

Yet Goddard was only an extreme example of almost every High Court judge I ever appeared before in a criminal case. Their summing up to the jury was invariably a second speech for the prosecution, more devastating because it came from a position of alleged impartiality.

Blatantly biased as Goddard was in his determination to get both prisoners convicted of murder, he was correct in law, as it stood then and as it stands now.

The Report of the Royal Commission on Capital Punishment 1949 – 1953 dealt, *inter alia*, with three situations:

(1) death caused by an act done in the commission of a felony;

(2) death caused to a peace officer in the course of resisting arrest;

(3) the position of accomplices.

It went back to the history of murder and referred to implied malice in three cases postulated by Coke:

(1) In respect of the manner of the deed. As if one killeth another without any provocation on the part of him that is slain the law implieth malice.

(2) In respect of the person slain. As if a magistrate or known officer, or any other that hath lawful warrant, and in doing or offering to do his office, or to execute his warrant, is slain, this is murder, by malice implied by law.

(3) In respect of the person killing. If A assault B to rob him, and in resisting A killeth B, this is murder by malice implied, albeit he – (A) never saw or knew him (B) before.

On the point of acts done in the commission of a felony, the Commission referred to the case of *R* v. *Jarmain* 1945 Cr. App. Rep. 39. The prisoner had entered a garage, intending to rob the proprietor, and found the cashier, a woman, counting the day's takings. According to his evidence, he pointed his loaded pistol at her and demanded the money. She went on writing for some moments and then said: 'Don't be silly.' He then transferred the pistol from his right to his left hand and, hoping to frighten her, cocked it twice, so that one live round was ejected, saying, 'This ain't no toy'. She only said, 'Don't be absurd.' He was disconcerted by her scornful attitude and, while he 'was thinking what to do', the pistol went off accidentally and killed her.

The Court of Criminal Appeal said:

We think that the object and scope of this branch of the law is at least this, that he who uses violent measures in the commission of a felony involving personal violence does so at his own risk, and is guilty of murder if those violent

183

measures result even inadvertently in the death of the victim.

For this purpose the use of a loaded firearm, in order to frighten the person victimized into submission, is a violent measure.

On the second point, the Commission wrote:

Stephen considered that a thief committed murder if he tripped up a pursuing policeman and the latter accidentally died. His statement of the law in the *Digest* was based on many old cases and authorities, including Coke and a fuller discussion of this subject in Hale's *Pleas of the Crown*, but he qualified it by expressing doubt whether it was still the law when he wrote in 1877.

Kenny indeed doubted whether so severe a rule had ever been established as the law, and pointed out that, in all the reported cases in which officers were killed, the actual means appear to have been 'intrinsically' dangerous.

However this may be, the case of *R* v. *Porter* clearly limited the old doctrine that any killing in the course of resisting arrest, however accidental, would be murder. In this case the prisoner and another man had been drinking at a public house and were taken into custody by a policeman on suspicion of stealing from the till. They submitted quietly to being handcuffed, but when the policeman tried to put Porter into a cart to take him to the police station, he resisted and there was a struggle. When the deceased man, a private person who was called upon by the policeman to assist him and was entitled to the same protection as the policeman himself, began to help in taking them away, Porter kicked him violently in the abdomen and he died two or three days later as a result of injuries caused by the kick.

The jury found the prisoner guilty only of manslaughter. The Commission concluded:

184

The distinction drawn between 'intention to inflict grievous harm' and 'intention to resist arrest', although on the facts of the particular case it may appear a distinction without a difference, was evidently intended to indicate that, in cases of resisting arrest, a blow intended to cause injury less than grievous bodily harm would justify a verdict of murder.

On the existing law, in 1952, I did well to get Lord Goddard, so far as Craig was concerned, to leave the verdict to the jury. Although he put the poison in in his summing up, without it, as was shown by the foreman asking for the jacket of Fairfax, they might well have convicted Craig only of manslaughter. On many previous occasions I had persuaded juries to apply their own concept of justice and not the law.

*

Bentley was a different case. About accomplices, the Commission wrote:

> All persons who take any part in the commission of a felony are in law felons; but at common law a distinction is drawn between principals in the first degree, principals in the second degree, accessories before the fact and accessories after the fact.
>
> *A principal in the first degree* is one who commits the offence with his own hands or through an innocent agent.
>
> *A principal in the second degree* is one who is present at the commission of an offence and aids and abets its commission.
>
> 'Presence' means only that at the material time he was at some place where he could give effective assistance to the commission of the offence.
>
> For example, if several persons agree to commit a burglary and one of them stays outside to keep watch, he is in law present at the commission of the offence and is a principal in the second degree. So too, A and B having agreed to rob C, with violence if necessary, if B waits in a

185

car near by while A commits the robbery, and afterwards A and B drive away together with the stolen property, B is a principal in the second degree to robbery.

If two persons agree, or one person procures another, to kill a third, the position is clear.

More difficult questions arise when the common purpose is only to commit a felony or to resist arrest, but death in fact results; but here too the law is well established.

If two persons agree to commit robbery with violence and one causes death while the other is present, actually or constructively, as a principal in the second degree, both are guilty of murder, although the latter had not specifically consented to such a degree of violence as was in fact used.

So also if two persons engage in the commission of crime, with a common resolution to resist by violence arrest by an officer of justice and one of them kills a policeman, it has been held that both are guilty of murder, and that it matters not that the violence contemplated by the accomplice who did not effect the killing was not extreme violence or violence sufficient to effect the object of their design at all costs.

However, once again, a jury might well have taken a different view of the role of Bentley. Undoubtedly he did not, and never would have, consented to the use of violence. As Craig told David Yallop, 'The gun didn't come into what we were going to do. If he'd thought that I was likely to get a gun out of my pocket he'd never have come out with me that night.' The real truth is that, far from inciting Craig to shoot, Bentley was doing all he could to stop him. Had these facts been before the jury, it is almost inevitable that they would have acquitted him.

*

Why then did not Frank Cassels make use of the vital evidence that I had given him that Bentley had come across to within six feet of Craig after Fairfax had been shot, to try to get the gun off him, and Craig had threatened to shoot him as well? That it

186

undoubtedly happened was what Craig told me at the time and what he confirmed eighteen years later when he was interviewed by David Yallop (see pp. 62–4 above).

I was not prepared to lead my client on this episode, since it showed him in a very bad light and was, in fact, totally destructive of his own defence. But I had got his permission to tell Frank Cassels and promise that he would not deny it if it was put to him in cross-examination. Indeed one of my main reasons for putting Craig in the witness box and running his defence was that this incident, which happened *before* PC Miles was shot, showed very clearly that, if there ever had been a joint venture, it had clearly come to an end with Bentley's arrest. The incident could have persuaded the jury not only that there had never in reality been a joint venture but that Bentley was actually trying to prevent Craig from firing.

Why did Frank not use this information? The simple reason is that his bloody fool of a client denied that it had ever happened, out of loyalty to his friend. He went to the opposite extreme in his evidence. His counsel asked:

What happened after you got behind the stack?
Sergeant Fairfax come and took me, sir, because I could not see nothing where I was standing and he come and took me, and walked me across the roof.
Sergeant Fairfax came and took you and walked you across the roof?
That is right.
When Sergeant Fairfax came and took you, did he say anything?
He said, 'I'm a police officer. I've got the place surrounded.'
When Sergeant Fairfax took hold of you, did you make any effort to struggle?
No, sir.
Or any attempt to strike him?
No.
What had happened between the time Sergeant Fairfax took hold of you and the time the first shot was fired?

Well, I do not know what happened on Christopher's side, sir, but Sergeant Fairfax had me and nothing happened. We just walked along the roof.

Did you break away from him once?

No, sir.

Up until the time a shot was fired did you know that Craig had a gun?

No, sir.

What happened when the shot was fired?

Sergeant Fairfax leaned on me and fell over like *that*. He did not touch the floor, though.

What did you do when the shot was fired?

I stood by Sergeant Fairfax.

You stood by Sergeant Fairfax?

Yes, sir.

Did you make any attempt to get away from him?

No, sir.

Did you make any attempt to strike him while he was on the ground, or while he was falling?

No.

After the shot was fired, did you see where Craig was standing?

Yes, sir, just a little way from the lift shaft.

Did you make any attempt to join Craig?

No.

What happened when Sergeant Fairfax recovered from the shock?

He got up – well, leaned up – and put me behind the staircase.

Did you make any attempt to get away from him?

No, sir.

Is it right, as he says, that he searched you and found the knuckleduster and the knife?

I gave him the knuckleduster; I took it out of my pocket myself.

From that time until you were taken downstairs by the police, did you remain behind the staircase head?

I did.

14. A Live Issue

If Bentley denied to his counsel, as he undoubtedly did, that the incident of his trying to get the gun off Craig had ever happened, he signed his own death warrant.

*

Ever since the trial, Iris Bentley, sister of Derek Bentley, has been seeking a posthumous royal pardon for her brother. In that, she is likely to be disappointed. But she is also campaigning for a public enquiry into the case. The Home Secretaries have so far refused that and, contrary to the normal rule that state papers are released after thirty years, have ordered that they should not be available to the public until the year 2047. In 1987 she applied to the Home Office to see the file relating to her brother's case. She was refused because, she was told by the Home Office, the file contained 'sensitive material'.

What would an enquiry reveal?

In my view it would reveal the original statements of McDonald, Fairfax and Harrison, which contain no reference whatsoever to Bentley's use of the words 'Let him have it, Chris'. It would also reveal the original statements of PCs Pain, Beecher-Brigden and Alderton, which contradict in important details the evidence of those police officers who gave evidence at the trial; as well as evidence about the firing of the actual bullet which killed PC Miles, which may well prove conclusively that it did not come from Craig's gun.

Terence Morris, in his *Crime and Criminal Justice since 1945*, observes in a footnote:

> The Craig and Bentley case raised – and still raises – important questions for both criminal jurisprudence and forensic criminology. Quite apart from whether Bentley should have been convicted, let alone hanged, doubts have even been raised about the veracity of the prosecution evidence about who fired the fatal shot. Some of these issues are discussed in H. Montgomery Hyde (ed.), *The Trial of Christopher Craig and Derek William Bentley* (London, 1954), which deals with legal aspects of the case,

189

and in a review of the book by J.E. Hall Williams in the *British Journal of Delinquency*, 6 (1954) no. 2.

Would an enquiry clear Bentley?

That is highly doubtful, given the notorious corruption of the English criminal system. The establishment is prone to appoint some Queen's Counsel who is greedy for judicial appointment and who will come up with a total whitewashing report. Scott Henderson QC did just that with the inquiry into the judicial murder of Timothy Evans, when he produced the ludicrous explanation that there were two necrophiliac murderers living in the same house in Rillington Place at the same time, unknown to one another, both burying bodies under the floor boards!

What no judicial inquiry will ever accept is that:

(1) the police habitually commit perjury;

(2) they habitually fabricate evidence against accused persons;

(3) they usually fabricate it in cases where they believe the accused to be guilty, but are quite happy to do it in cases where they know perfectly well that the accused is innocent, as with Stephen Ward, who was involved in the Profumo case, or all the unfortunate Irish men and women known, as the Guildford Four, the Maguire Seven and the Birmingham Six;

(4) that they and previous Directors of Public Prosecutions and prosecuting counsel deliberately suppress and conceal evidence in favour of the defence (I say nothing about Allan Green, the present DPP who, for a change, appears to be an honest man);

(5) that the police extract false confessions out of the accused by methods ranging from deceit to torture – one of the Birmingham Six was known to the others as 'shit his

pants', because that is just what he did when he was so beaten up and terrorised that he signed a false confession;

(6) judges are, and have always been, mere servile tools of the executive, whether that be a monarch or an elected dictatorship – witness Lord Donaldson's refusal to apply the law of *habeas corpus* in 1991 to innocent Iraqis resident in this country during the Gulf War;

(7) in many criminal trials, the judge's summing up is nothing more than a second prosecution speech, more effective because it professes to be delivered from a position of professional impartiality;

(8) defence counsel are habitually harassed at every turn, as Frank Cassels and I were.

*

Will Iris Bentley secure the exoneration of her brother? Even if she were to secure an inquiry, it is more than certain that it would not conclude that he had been wrongfully convicted. For the attitude of lawyers is embodied in Gilbert's lines:

The law is the true embodiment of everything that's excellent. It has no kind of fault or flaw.

As a Conservative Member of Parliament, R.M. Bell QC, told the House of Commons several years ago:

The chief contemporary threat to freedom comes from the judges.

And as Edward Hyde, Lord Chancellor and first Earl of Clarendon, wrote on 22 May 1641:

Good God! How have accused persons these late years been punished, when the Judges themselves have been such delinquents.

191

Index

Index

Index